Presented To:

_____

_____

From:

_____

_____

Date:

_____

_____

To June with many
thanks.

Marie

Coffee Break
with God

HB
HONOR
B O O K S

Tulsa, Oklahoma

8th Printing

Coffee Break with God
ISBN 1-56292-034-0
Copyright © 1996 by Honor Books, Inc.
P.O. Box 55388
Tulsa, Ok 74155

Manuscript prepared by W. B. Freeman Concepts, Inc., Tulsa, Oklahoma.
Cover Illustration by Taylor Bruce

Gimme a Break!

"*Gimme* a break" has been a popular phrase in American culture for more than two decades now. And the fact is that now more than ever, we need a break!

Often, our day does not go as we planned. Problems emerge and demand solutions. Questions arise and require answers. Conflicts erupt and we must settle them. Situations shift and we must adjust. New opportunities come our way and we find ourselves making tough decisions.

Few days go as smoothly as we would like!

In the midst of the chaos we can take a momentary break. No matter how frantic the schedule or desperate the situation, we can turn to God's Word for strength and wisdom. There is simply no better break than one that pulls us away from trouble and draws us closer to the Answer, the Lord Jesus Christ.

He alone can give us the truth, courage to stick with our priorities and get back on track if we have erred, peace that passes our understanding, and perspective marked by faith, hope, and love. He alone can provide a powerful word for our hearts that speaks to whatever we are facing.

No one may "give" you a break today, but you can give yourself one. In the middle of your day, give yourself a *Coffee Break With God*!

Running Persistently

It is God who arms me with strength and makes my way
perfect. He makes my feet like the feet of a deer;
he enables me to stand on the heights.
2 Samuel 22:33-34

Bob Kempainen was determined to make the 1996 U.S. Men's Olympic marathon team. He was willing to go to any lengths, no matter how gut-wrenching.

On a hilly course in Charlotte, North Carolina, he won the trials — but was sick five times in the last two miles.

Kempainen, the American record-holder in the marathon, has experienced stomach troubles since junior high school. But that hasn't kept this medical student from pursuing marathoning.

"To stop was out of the question," he said, when asked about his physical condition. With the goal in sight, he knew there would be plenty of time to rest after the race and five months to prepare for Atlanta.

When God puts a desire in your heart to achieve a specific goal, you can have the confidence that He will give you the strength and the ability to accomplish it.

Every person has their own obstacles to overcome in life. In Kempainen's case, the condition of his stomach is trying to hinder him from winning the marathon race at the Olympics. In your life it will be something else. But we all face difficulties and challenges on the road to success — and the difference between those who succeed and those who fail is simply persistence.

Life is not a level, smooth path, but rather a series of hills and valleys. There are times spent on the mountain top, when everything seems clear and perfect. Then there are those times when we feel like we're wandering around in a dark cavern, feeling our way along and trusting God for every step of faith.

A runner gets a "second wind" after forcing himself to go on when he feels like he can't. We feel the joy of God's Spirit lift us up and carry us on when we choose to continue in faith, no matter how we feel or what's going on around us.

Take a moment and set your heart to be persistent in your faith — faith in God to lead you, pick you up when you have fallen, give you strength to go on, and ultimately bring you to victory.

What to Do

But if any of you lacks wisdom, let him ask of God,
who gives to all men generously and without reproach,
and it will be given to him.
James 1:5 NASB

An ancient Jewish story tells of a young traveler, who encountered an old man at the edge of a forest. Staring into the darkness of the overgrown foliage in front of him, the young man asked his elder, "Can you tell me the best way through this forest?"

The wise old man replied, "I cannot."

The young man asked, "But haven't you lived here for awhile? Surely you have been in the forest many times."

"Yes," the old man said, "and I can tell you all of the pitfalls and dangers I have encountered. I can tell you which paths *not* to take. But I have never been all the way through the forest. That is something you must experience for yourself."

What to Do

Every day, we encounter all kinds of problems which others may have faced before us. It is a good thing to ask for advice in these matters. In truth, however, every set of problems has its own unique twists and turns. These subtle differences make each situation unique.

The best advice others give us may very well fall into the category of things "not to do." We can learn from the mistakes of others, and from our own, but in the end, the solution to *our* new and specific problem will be new and unique.

It is critical, therefore, for us to rely upon the counsel of the Lord every hour of the day, and to ask specifically for His wisdom as we face questions, needs, or troubles. He knows the precise answer for the particular circumstance we face. He knows the beginning from the end!

Others may be experts at what *not* to do, or what is a *good* thing to do, but only the Lord can point us in the direction of what is *best* to do.

During this short break, ask the Lord to show you the *best* way to handle your day.

Staying Charged Up

Let the people renew their strength.
Isaiah 41:1 KJV

The age we live in has been described as the age of the to-do list that can't be done. Facing overwhelming demands, it's hard to give ourselves permission to rest or take a break. But the rewards — renewed perspective, clearer insight, physical energy, spiritual preparedness — are well worth it.

Before automatic headlight controls were installed in automobiles, it was easy to park a car and leave the headlights on. Perhaps we were in a hurry or it was light enough outside that we forgot we had turned the lights on. If we were gone for very long we returned to find the car battery dead. To get the car running again, the battery had to be recharged.

Just like a car battery, our own supply of energy is not infinite. We must replenish it frequently with sleep, rest, food, and relaxation. Our busy nonstop days can be draining. Operating at top speed, we utilize all available emotional, physical, mental, and spiritual resources. Before we know it, our energy is consumed.

Unless we pay careful attention, we will drain our "battery" to the point of feeling "dead on our feet." Being fatigued can cause our perception to be distorted and our responses to others to be negative. Furthermore, if we fail to do something about it, over time it can result in physical or emotional illness.

Charles Spurgeon, a well-known 19th-century preacher said, "Without constant restoration we are not ready for the perpetual assaults. If we allow the good in our lives to get weak — or our 'light' to grow dim — the evil will surely gather strength and struggle desperately for the mastery over us."

You are wise to take a short break now and then during the day — and to turn off your lights when you to go bed at night! Living this way will help you to maintain your energy supply and enable you to be more productive and content.

Along the Way

See how the lilies of the field grow. They do not labor or spin.
Yet I tell you that not even Solomon in all his splendor
was dressed like one of these.
Matthew 6:28-29

Scottish explorer Mungo Park made quite a name for himself, though he lived only 35 years in the late 1700s. During his short stay on earth, he managed to have the kind of adventures from which legends are made.

His studies of plant and animal life in Sumatra brought him to the attention of the African Association. Consequently, they funded his expedition to explore the true course of the Niger River.

Hampered by perilous fevers, lack of supplies, and even imprisonment, Park completed only part of his journey before he was forced to quit. He returned to Britain and wrote a book about his adventures.

Ernest Hemingway eventually retold one of Park's stories. Park was lost and alone in the African desert and had resigned himself to die. Then he saw it: a beautiful moss-flower. The plant was only as big as one of his fingers, but he was overcome with admiration for its symmetry.

Encountering this wonder in the middle of his crisis, he reflected, "Can the Being who planted, watered, and brought to perfection, in this obscure part of the world, a thing which appears of so small importance, look with unconcern upon the situation and suffering of creatures formed after His own image?" he asked. "Surely not."

Thus encouraged, and putting aside his hunger and fatigue, Park rose and made his way to relief. We can draw inspiration from his example. He was a man who knew how to appreciate the simple things in life — and their Creator.

In your most trying moments today, look for a moss-flower! Remember how much more your Heavenly Father cares for you, and how He loves to provide your every need.

Take a Breather

*And the Lord God formed man of the dust of the ground,
and breathed into his nostrils the breath of life.*
Genesis 2:7 NKJV

The fast-paced, relentless duties of life often
cause us to declare with a sigh, "I need a breather." We
may be voicing more truth than we realize!

Medical researchers have discovered that for
virtually every person who *works* — whether at
physically demanding manual labor or intellectually
demanding white-collar labor — performance level
improves when a person breathes properly.

Good breathing is defined as regular, deep, and
slow. The opposite — "shallow, rapid, and uneven" —
is a sure sign to most physicians that something is
seriously wrong.

Good breathing is essential for good health. It
supplies oxygen to the bloodstream, which is vital for

the functioning of all bodily organs, especially the heart and brain.

The Scriptures tell us God breathes His life into us both physically and spiritually. Jesus breathed upon His disciples to impart the Holy Spirit to them (John 20:22). The early church experienced the Holy Spirit as a rushing mighty wind — a manifestation of the breath of God (Acts 2:1-2).

Today in our personal lives, an awareness of the Spirit of God working in us is often experienced as a fresh breeze, one that cleanses and revives us in every part of our being. The word "inspiration" literally means to have the things of the Spirit put *into us*.

We do well to take a periodic "breather" in the Lord's presence. When we do, we find the rhythm of our life evens out. We find our spirits are refreshed and renewed at a level deeper than the superficiality of our daily routine.

Pause to receive from the Lord, and see if you don't find yourself slowing down and releasing the tensions of fear, frustration, and futility. You will be able to think more clearly, God's love can flow more freely, and creative ideas will begin to fill your mind.

Take a breather! Inhale deeply of His goodness, strength, and love.

Editing Your Life

*Wherefore seeing we also are compassed about with so great a
cloud of witnesses, let us lay aside every weight,
and the sin which doth so easily beset us.*
Hebrews 12:1 KJV

Disney films are known the world over as the best in animation, but the studio didn't earn that reputation easily. One of the reasons for the level of excellence achieved was the filmmaker himself. Walt Disney was ruthless about cutting anything that got in the way of the unfolding story.

Ward Kimball, one of the animators for *Snow White*, recalls working 240 days on a four-minute sequence. The dwarfs made soup for Snow White, almost destroying the kitchen in the process. Disney thought it was funny, but he decided the scene interrupted the flow of the picture, so it was edited out.

Often we find ourselves doing "good" things which are not only unnecessary, but a distraction from the unfolding story of our lives. Like the soup scene, many of these things are worthwhile or entertaining, but they lack the essential elements of being the best we can do with the time and talents God has given us.

In some cases, life can become so crowded with these "commitments," we don't have room for the essential things God wants to do through us.

The next time you're asked to take on another "good scene," ask yourself:

- Does this fit in with the plan God has set before me — do I have a lasting inner peace about it?

- Will this task help me or others grow closer to the Lord?

- Can I do this without taking away from the time I've already committed to my family, church, job, or friends?

As you pause to consider the rest of today, consider this: When the film of your life is shown, will it be as great as it might have been? A lot will depend on the multitude of *good* things you edit out of your life in favor of the *great* things God wants to do through you!

Life's Essence

For as he thinketh in his heart, so is he.
Proverbs 23:7 KJV

Ben Patterson writes in *The Grand Essentials*:
"*I have a theory about old age...I believe that when life has whittled us down, when joints have failed and skin has wrinkled and capillaries have clogged and hardened, what is left of us will be what we were all along, in our essence.*

"*Exhibit A is a distant uncle...All his life he did nothing but find new ways to get rich...He spent his senescence very comfortably, drooling and babbling constantly about the money he had made...When life whittled him down to his essence, all there was left was raw greed. This is what he had cultivated in a thousand little ways over a lifetime.*

"*Exhibit B is my wife's grandmother....When she died in her mid-eighties, she had already been senile for several years. What did this lady talk about? The best example I can think of was when we asked her to pray before dinner. She would reach out and hold the hands of those sitting beside her, a broad, beatific smile would spread across her face, her dim eyes would fill with tears as she looked up to heaven, and her chin would quaver as she poured out her love to Jesus.*

" That was Edna in a nutshell. She loved Jesus and she loved people. She couldn't remember our names, but she couldn't keep her hands from patting us lovingly whenever we got near her. When life whittled her down to her essence, all there was left was love: love for God and love for others."[1]

The difference in the "essence" that emerged as life waned for each of these people is defined by the priorities each person chose as he or she went about the day's business.

Grandma Edna did all that she did each day because of her love for her family and her love for God and His children. The uncle's life was lived only for himself.

When life has whittled you to your essence, whom will you most resemble: the uncle or the grandmother?

What Shape Are You In?

The inward man is being renewed day by day.
2 Corinthians 4:16 NKJV

Clay pots of all shapes and sizes were valuable tools in ancient households. Large jars were used to store water and olive oil, jugs were used to carry water, and small terra-cotta vials held perfume. Clay storage jars were filled with grain and other foods. Homemakers used clay pots for cooking. At mealtime, shallow pottery bowls were used as platters and dishes. In the evening the homes were lit by clay lamps.

The potters who supplied these much-needed pots were important to the economic life of ancient villages. A modern potter described her craft like this:

"Both my hands shaped this pot. And, the place where it actually forms is a place of tension between the pressure applied from the outside and the pressure of the hand on *the inside. That's the way my life has been. Sadness and death and misfortune and the love of friends and all the things that happened to me that I didn't even choose. All of that influenced my life. But, there are things I believe in about myself, my faith in God and the love of some friends that worked on the insides of me. My life, like this pot, is the result of what happened on the outside and what was going on inside of me. Life, like this pot, comes to be in places of tension."*[2]

Throughout the day we may be buffeted by stress, pulled apart by responsibilities, and pressed by challenges that come at us from the outside. Without strength of spirit on the inside, those difficulties will cause us to collapse under the external pressure.

During this break, feed your spirit with Scripture. This will keep you strong, renewed, and restored *within*. You can respond with inner strength and creativity to what could otherwise defeat you.

Remember, your inner life gives you the strength you need to become a useful vessel in the household of God.

Use That Powerful Engine!

It is God who arms me with strength
and makes my way perfect.
Psalm 18:32

What a pleasure it is to drive a car with a powerful engine on a level highway. Picture a sunny day when there's no traffic and you're not in a hurry to get anywhere. You sing along with your favorite music tape and enjoy driving solely for driving's sake.

We are more likely to find ourselves in a much less powerful vehicle, however, climbing a series of steep hills...in the rain...with lots of traffic behind us and in front of us...and late for an appointment.

But is it possible to ride the rougher road and have the same peace and tranquillity inside as when we drive the level highway? The Bible says it is.

The difference is simply the powerful engine, which makes the hills seem less steep and rush hour less tedious. It's a lot easier to keep moving steadily through traffic when you have a continuous hum from the motor, instead of lurching, dying, starting...lurching, dying, starting...in your own strength.

God is our powerful engine. He makes the difficult highway become manageable.

Perhaps your day started out smoothly, but by now you've left the easy stretch of road and come to the rolling hills. Now more than ever is the time to remind yourself that your Father in heaven loves you and wants to help you.

With God's strength, you can stay alert and focused, maintaining an even pace and an even temperament regardless of the challenge. He will help you work through any problems that arise without compromising your integrity. He may even show you some short cuts — and the gas mileage is great!

All you have to do is ask God to strengthen you and get back on the road. Before you know it, you will be on the mountain top with a clear view!

Through the Maze

*We have this treasure in earthen vessels, that the excellence of
the power may be of God and not of us.*
2 Corinthians 4:7 NKJV

*I*hara Saikuku, the author of two enduring
works, *The Japanese Family Storehouse* and *The
Millionaire's Gospel* had this to say about the challenge
we all face in the pursuit of personal success:

"*T*o *be born thus empty into this modern age, this
mixture of good and ill, and yet to steer through life on an
honest course to the splendors of success — this is a feat
reserved for paragons of our kind, a task beyond the
nature of the normal man.*"

Interestingly, Saikuku was writing more than three
hundred years ago! He lived from 1642 to 1693. His
statement confirms the familiar axiom, "Nothing ever
changes." What was true about human nature three
hundred years ago is still true today.

Each one of us is born into what may be likened to a maze — with many options for false starts, unproductive detours, and dead ends. The person who makes wise choices and decisions is the one most likely to make it through the maze of life with greatest efficiency, ease, and productivity.

The analogy of a maze holds true for each *day* also. In any given day we face numerous opportunities to make a wrong turn or give in to temptation instead of taking that big leap of faith to continue in God's plan for our life.

The Scriptures would agree with Saikuku that steering an honest course is "beyond the nature of the normal man." Rather than an attribute of the unusual or specially-gifted person, however, this ability to make good moral choices is regarded by the Scriptures as evidence of the Holy Spirit at work in a person's life. It is the Spirit who helps us choose good and refuse evil.

Whenever you are faced with a decision today, ask the Holy Spirit to guide you. Ask Him to show you the way through today's maze!

Faulty Assumptions

*The pride of thine heart hath deceived thee, thou that dwellest
in the clefts of the rock, whose habitation is high; that saith in
his heart, Who shall bring me down to the ground?*
Obadiah 1:3 KJV

A traveler at an airport went to a lounge and bought a small package of cookies to eat while reading a newspaper. Gradually, she became aware of a rustling noise. Looking from behind her paper, she was flabbergasted to see a neatly dressed man helping himself to her cookies. Not wanting to make a scene, she leaned over and took a cookie herself.

A minute or two passed, and then she heard more rustling. He was helping himself to another cookie! By this time, they had come to the end of the package. She was angry but didn't dare allow herself to say anything. Then, as if to add insult to injury, the man broke the remaining cookie in two, pushed half across to her, ate the other half, and left.

Still fuming later when her flight was announced, the woman opened her handbag to get her ticket. To her shock and embarrassment, there was her pack of unopened cookies!

It's so easy to make assumptions about what is happening around us. We expect things to be a certain way based on past experience, what we know, or have been told about a situation. Assumptions are not always wrong, but they are never to be trusted. Too many times they lead to embarrassment and even destruction.

The Bible tells us that assumption is based on human reasoning and the driving force behind it is pride. As the verse above says, it is pride — we think we know everything — which allows us to be deceived.

Pride caused the woman in this story to assume she was right and the gentleman was wrong. Instead of seeing him through God's eyes and praying for wisdom to handle the situation God's way, she ignored the man. In the end, she was completely blind to his kindness toward her.

When you find yourself in a conflict with others, avoid prideful assumptions by walking in God's love. See other people and situations through His eyes. After all, your vision is limited, but He knows exactly what's going on!

Give It to God

Casting all your care upon him; for he careth for you.
1 Peter 5:7

*V*ery often it's not the crises of life that get to us, but the little things that wear us down. We can learn a lesson from the oyster:

*T*here once was an oyster whose story I tell,
Who found that sand had got under his shell;
Just one little grain, but it gave him much pain,
For oysters have feelings although they're so plain.
Now, did he berate the working of Fate,
Which had led him to such a deplorable state?
Did he curse out the government, call for an election?
No; as he lay on the shelf, he said to himself:
"If I cannot remove it, I'll try to improve it."
So the years rolled by as the years always do,
And he came to his ultimate destiny — stew.
And this small grain of sand which had bothered him so,

Give It to God

Was a beautiful pearl, all richly aglow.
Now this tale has a moral — for isn't it grand
What an oyster can do with a morsel of sand?
What couldn't we do if we'd only begin
With all of the things that get under our skin?[3]

How does an irritating grain of sand become a pearl? Author Elizabeth Elliot has insight about adversities both large and small: Give it to God.

"If the only thing you have to offer is a broken heart, you offer a broken heart....Simply give it to Him as the little boy gave Jesus his five loaves and two fishes — with the same feeling of the disciples when they said, 'What is the good of that for such a crowd?'

"In almost anything I offer to Christ, my reaction would be, 'what is the good of that?' The use He makes of it is none of my business; it is His business, it is His blessing. Whatever it is, which at the moment is God's means of testing my faith and bringing me to the recognition of who He is — that is the thing I can offer."[4]

The Spice of Life

Because of the Lord's great love we are not consumed,
for his compassions never fail. They are new every
morning; great is your faithfulness.
Lamentations 3:22-23

Most of us have a routine we follow every morning. There's also a certain routine for our jobs, and another one that takes over after work. Even on the weekends, there are things that must be done.

Have you come to dread another sink full of dishes, another load of laundry, another car to wash, another lawn to mow, another rug to vacuum, or another floor to scrub? Is there any end to the "routine" of life?

There's no getting out of most of those chores. Someone has to keep things clean and running smoothly. The one thing we *can* control is our attitude toward it all.

Rather than emphasizing the "same old," we should remember what the Bible says: "if anyone is in

Christ, he is a new creation; the old has gone, the new has come!" (2 Corinthians 5:17) and, "I will give you a new heart and put a new spirit in you" (Ezekiel 36:26).

God never changes, but He loves variety. He wants us to embrace life and keep our eyes open for new possibilities, our minds open to new ideas, our hearts open to new people who cross our path.

Even in the midst of the "same old same old" daily routine, He can bring something new, unusual, and different. Sometimes upsetting the routine can be distressing. But don't let it shake your confidence in God's plan for your life, let it enhance His plan.

This morning, be aware that whether life seems to have a "sameness" or has turned chaotic, you are always changing inside. Through it all, the Lord is continually stirring new life within you, giving you new dreams and goals, and molding you to be more like Jesus today!

Hold On!

Preserve me, O God, for in You I put my trust.
Psalm 16:1 NKJV

A little girl was very nervous at the prospect of her first horseback ride, even though she was to be perched behind her grandfather, who was an excellent rider. As her parents helped her onto the horse, she cried, "What do I do? I don't know how to ride a horse! I haven't done this before! What do I do?"

Her grandfather said in a reassuring tone, "Don't worry about the horse or about how to ride it. Just hold on to me, darlin', just hold on to me."

What good advice for us today! We thought our day was going to be a "tired-old-nag" sort of day, but it turned out to be a "bucking-bronco" day instead. On days like that, we need to "just hold on" to our faith in the Lord and stay in the saddle.

Hold On!

One of the foremost ways in which we hold on to the Lord is through constant communication with Him — a continual flow of prayer and praise. We can pray in any place at any time. Even a "thought" prayer turns our will and focus toward the Lord and puts our trust in Him. It is when we lose touch with the Lord that we are in danger of "falling" into panic and the frustration, frenzy, and failure that can come with it.

The Lord knows the end from the beginning of each day, and He knows how long the current upheaval in your life will last. Above all, He knows how to bring you safely through each "wild ride" keeping you in His divine peace all the way.

Harriet Beecher Stowe offered this advice:

"When you get in a tight place and everything goes against you, till it seems you could not hold on a minute longer, never give up then, for that is just the place and time that the tide will turn."

Always remember that you don't "ride" the beasts of this life alone. The Lord is with you, and He has the reins firmly in His grasp. Just hold on!

The Still, Small Voice

My conscience is clear, but that does not make me innocent.
It is the Lord who judges me.
1 Corinthians 4:4

In his book, *Focus on the Family*, Rolf Zettersten writes about his good friend, Edwin, who bought a new car. The car had lots of extra features — among them was a recording of a soft female voice, which gently reminded him if he had failed to fasten his seat belt or was running low on fuel. Appropriately, Edwin dubbed the voice "the little woman."

On one of his many road trips, "the little woman" began informing him that he needed to stop and fill his tank with gasoline. "Your fuel level is low," she cooed in her soft voice. Edwin nodded his head knowingly and thanked her with a smile. He decided, however, that he had enough gas to take him at least another 50 miles, so he kept on driving.

The problem was, in only a few minutes the little lady spoke the warning again — and again and again and again until Edwin was ready to scream. Even though he knew, logically, that the recording was simply repeating itself, it really seemed as though the little woman spoke more and more insistently each time.

Finally he'd had all he could take. He pulled to the side of the road and, after a quick search under the dashboard for the appropriate wires, gave them a good yank. *So much for the little woman, he thought.*

He was still feeling very smug for having had the last say when his car began missing and coughing. He had run out of gas! Somewhere inside the dashboard, he was almost certain he could hear the laughter of a woman!

Our manufacturer, God, has given us a factory-installed warning voice. It's called the conscience. Sometimes we may think it's a nuisance, overly insistent, or just plain wrong. However, most of us will learn sooner or later that it is often trying to tell us exactly what we need to know.

Whether you are being told to stop for gas or being warned not to turn off the main road, your conscience knows what is right. Follow it today and see if you don't experience more peace about every decision you make.

Energy Crisis

The joy of the Lord is your strength.
Nehemiah 8:10 KJV

*M*ost of us have a daily routine — a series of repetitious chores, errands, and tasks that demand our time and are required to maintain life at its most basic level. "Routine," says Jewish theologian Abraham Heschel, "makes us resistant to wonder." When we let our sense of wonder and awe drain away we lose the sense of our preciousness to God.

Jesus recognized our preoccupation with these duties in His Sermon on the Mount. He said, "Do not worry about your life, what you will eat or drink; or about your body, what you will wear. Is not life more important than food, and the body more important than clothes?" (Matthew 6:25).

But how do we apprehend the life that is "more important than food" when so much of our time and energy are spent providing and maintaining the essentials of food, clothing, and shelter? The "daily grind" can cause us to lose our sense of God's purpose and presence. We may feel like Job, who despaired, "When he passes me, I cannot see him; when he goes by, I cannot perceive him" (Job 9:11).

Julian of Norwich, the 14th-century English mystic, had a perspective that can help restore joy to even the most lackluster days. She said, "Joy is to see God in everything." The psalmist wrote, "The heavens declare the glory of God" (Psalm 19:1 KJV), and the prophet Isaiah writes, "The whole earth is full of his glory" (Isaiah 6:3 KJV). The glory of creation is that it points us to the greater glory of the Creator.

If life's routines are wearing down your enthusiasm and joy, take time to seek out His love, majesty, and goodness revealed in creation. Be renewed in your joy of who God is — and who you are to Him — and find His strength and purpose in even your most routine tasks.

Easy as A, B, C

For in the day of trouble he will keep me safe in his dwelling;
he will hide me in the shelter of his tabernacle
and set me high upon a rock.
Psalm 27:5

"We need to run some tests." Those are words you never want to hear from a doctor. Inundated as we are with medical bulletins, our first inclination is to expect the worst.

Especially intimidating are the machines used to diagnose our disorders. The Magnetic Resonance Imager (MRI), with its oh-so-narrow magnetic metal tunnel, can bring out the claustrophobe in all of us.

A test like this causes a real break in our daily routine. (Have you noticed that most of them are scheduled in the morning?) While we might never reach the point where we look forward to such "breaks," we can do what one woman did to use the time constructively.

Once inside the tube, she found herself on the verge of panic. Then she remembered some advice her pastor had given her: When things are going badly for you, pray for someone else.

To simplify things, she decided to pray alphabetically. Several friends whose names began with A immediately came to mind. She prayed for Albert's sore knee, Amy's decision about work, and Andrew's upcoming final exams. She moved on to B and continued through the alphabet. By the letter D she was totally oblivious to her environment.

Thirty minutes later, she was only halfway through the alphabet and the test was done. A day later, she used a short "break" in her doctor's office to complete her prayers while she waited for the test results, which showed no abnormalities.

Not all breaks are of our own design. Some are forced upon us and seem very unpleasant. But what we do with them is up to us.

When you find yourself taking a break from your routine that would not be your chosen activity, turn it over to your Father God and watch Him transform it into a special time for the two of you.

The Return on Giving

Give, and it will be given to you; good measure, pressed down,
shaken together, and running over.
Luke 6:38 NKJV

A drowning man gestured frantically to a man standing at the edge of a swimming pool. Splashing his way until he was within arm's reach of the side of the pool, the drowning man hollered: "Here, let me give you my hand." The man reached down into the water, took the outstretched hand, and pulled the distressed man to safety. Afterward the lifesaver told the man he had rescued, "I find it unusual that you said 'Let me give you my hand,' rather than asking me to give you my hand."

The rescued man replied, "I work for a charitable organization, sir. I've discovered that people are always more willing to receive than they are to give!"

While the tendency of our human nature may be to receive more than to give, the Gospel tells us giving is actually the most productive way to receive! Whatever we extend to others, give to others, or do for others comes back to us multiplied. This principle has been recognized by the business community. Donald David has said:

You never get promoted when no one else knows your current job. The best basis for being advanced is to organize yourself out of every job you're put in. Most people are advanced because they're pushed up from people underneath them rather than pulled by the top."

Find ways to give to those around you today. Especially to those who may be in subordinate positions. Freely share information with them and be generous in your praise and encouragement. Give advice on how to do specific tasks more quickly, more efficiently, or with greater quality. You will find that the more you do to help others in their work, the easier your own workload will become.

Another Point of View

So we say with confidence, "The Lord is my helper;
I will not be afraid. What can man do to me?"
Hebrews 13:6

On July 15, 1986, Roger Clemens, the sizzling right-hander for the Boston Red Sox, started his first All-Star Game. In the second inning he came to bat, something he hadn't done in years because of the American League's designated-hitter rule. He took a few uncertain practice swings and then looked out at his forbidding opponent, Dwight Gooden, who had won the Cy Young Award the previous year.

Gooden wound up and threw a white-hot fastball that flew right by Clemens. With an embarrassed smile on his face, Clemens stepped out of the box and asked catcher Gary Carter, "Is that what my pitches look like?"

"You bet it is!" replied Carter. Although Clemens quickly struck out, he went on to pitch three perfect innings and was named the game's most valuable player. With a fresh reminder of how overpowering a good fastball is, he later said from that day on he pitched with far greater boldness.

Occasionally we forget the power we have at our disposal when it comes to speaking the Gospel of Jesus Christ. Maybe we need to step to the other side of the plate for a moment to be reminded!

The Holy Spirit within us always provides a powerful witness. We can "pitch" the Gospel with the confidence and authority that God has given us. But too many times, we weakly toss out a word here and there about Jesus, hoping not to make too great a stir. After all, we don't want to be too pushy, politically incorrect, or called a fanatic! We step up to the plate of opportunity without real conviction. Is it any wonder we seem to have no impact?

If you have an opportunity today, tell someone about how Jesus has changed your life with the conviction and power that comes from your heart. This is the power of the Holy Spirit within you. Then have peace in knowing you have done your part, and the rest is up to Him!

With Attitude

Whatever you do, do all to the glory of God.
1 Corinthians 10:31 RSV

"*To* love what you do and feel that it matters — how could anything be more fun?" asks Katharine Graham. That's what we all desire, isn't it?

No matter what work we do, our attitude toward our work is vital to our basic sense of self-worth. The ideal for everyone is to love the work they do and feel that it has significance. While no job is enjoyable or pleasant all the time, it is possible to derive satisfaction from what we bring to a job — the attitude with which we perform our tasks.

For example, Brother Lawrence, the 17th-century Carmelite, found joy in his job washing dishes at the monastery. In the monotony of his routine work he found the opportunity to focus on God and feel His presence.

Modern-day entrepreneurs Ben Cohen and Jerry Greenfield make and sell ice cream with a purpose. The bottom line of Ben & Jerry's Homemade, Inc., is "How much money is left over at the end of the year?" and "How have we improved life in the community?"

"Leftover money" goes to fund Ben & Jerry's Foundation, which distributes funds to worthy nonprofit causes. These are charities that help needy children, preserve the Amazonian rain forest, provide safe shelter for emotionally or psychologically distressed people, and fund a business staffed by unemployed homeless people. By helping others with their profits, Ben and Jerry put more *meaning* into their ice cream business.

The Scriptures teach that all service ranks the same with God, because it is not *what* you do that matters, but the *spirit* in which you do it. A street sweeper who does his work to serve God and bless the people who travel on the streets is as pleasing to Him as the priest or pastor who teaches and nurtures their congregations.

If you feel your work is insignificant, ask God to open your eyes! When you do all for Him and to serve others, no task is unimportant!

Counting the Cost

*For which of you, intending to build a tower,
sitteth not down first, and counteth the cost,
whether he have sufficient to finish it?*
Luke 14:28 KJV

Imagine a natural disaster strikes your town and destroys everyone's home, as well as all the businesses, community services, recreation areas, and houses of worship. The government predicts that it will take nearly a decade to rebuild.

That's what happened to Valmeyer, Illinois, during the 1993 Midwest floods. People who had been neighbors for most of their lives lost everything except their determination to stick together. So they decided to start over and rebuild together — in record time.

To accomplish such a monumental task, people had to step away from their normal lives and commit to new tasks. After all, there were buildings to construct, federal and state funds to secure, and utilities and social services to restore. An entire town had to be relocated and rebuilt from the ground up.

In this case, a little motivation went a long way. The $22 million project was to be completed by the end of 1996 — barely three years after the flood. The statement by Helen Keller, "Every day we should do a little more than is required," could have been the motto of the people of Valmeyer. They took that sentiment to heart and rebuilt their town.[5]

Is there something in your life that you could accomplish much sooner by "counting the cost" and then doing a little extra every day, every week, or every month? Financial advisers tell us that home mortgages can be paid off years in advance by adding only $100 a month to the principal payment. Faster weight loss can be achieved by cutting out just 100 extra calories a day. Every project seems to have a momentum that is accelerated when we do "just a little more."

Focus on something that is important to you and then map out a strategy for an "extra" touch.

Balm

Is there no balm in Gilead, is there no physician there?
Jeremiah 8:22 NKJV

In centuries past, groves of balsam trees were planted on terraces in the hills south of Jerusalem. They were also planted in fields east of the Jordan River, in the area known as Gilead. The sap from the trees was harvested to create a balm that was considered to have great medicinal value in helping wounds to heal. The balm was used especially to treat scorpion stings and snake bites. Since scorpions and snakes abounded in the wilderness regions of Judea and throughout the Middle East, the balm was extremely valuable and was an important export item along ancient trade routes.[6]

The "balm of Gilead" is identified with Jesus. He is the One Who heals our wounds.

Every day holds the potential for us to experience stings and bites, both literal and figurative. While not always life-threatening, these "jabs" from the enemy are hurtful nonetheless. How can we apply the balm of Jesus Christ to them?

The foremost way is through praise. Any time we find ourselves under attack or wounded, we can turn our minds and hearts to Him with a word, a thought, or a song of praise.

For example, if we feel attacked by a swarm of stinging problems, we can say, "Praise You, Jesus, You are my Deliverer, my Rescuer, my sure Help." If we feel wounded by a failure, we can say, "Praise You, Jesus, You are my Redeemer."

If we feel wounded in the heart by a word of criticism or rejection, we can say, "Praise You, Jesus, You have sent the Holy Spirit to be my Comforter." If we feel overwhelmed by too many responsibilities, we can say, "Praise You, Jesus, You are my Prince of Peace."

As you praise Jesus, you will find the pain associated with an incident or situation soothed. He is the Lord of lords — including anything that tries to "lord" it over you!

The Guide

And the Lord shall guide thee continually, and satisfy
thy soul in drought, and make fat thy bones:
and thou shalt be like a watered garden, and like
a spring of water, whose waters fail not.
Isaiah 58:11 KJV

Foreigners who wish to explore the wilderness areas of South America alone must be well prepared to face a number of challenges. Those venturing into the Amazon jungles or Andes Mountains without a guide or adequate preparation will quickly find their lives in peril.

In *A Slow and Certain Light*, missionary Elisabeth Elliot tells of two adventurers who stopped by to see her at her mission station. Loaded heavily with equipment for the rain forest, they sought no advice. They merely asked her to teach them a few phrases of the language so they might converse a bit with the Indians.

The Guide

Amazed at their temerity, she saw a parallel between these travelers and Christians. She writes: "Sometimes we come to God as the two adventurers came to me — confident and, we think, well-informed and well-equipped. But has it occurred to us that with all our accumulation of stuff, something is missing?"

She suggests that, in our own arrogance, we often ask God for far too little. "We know what we need — a yes or no answer, please, to a simple question. Or perhaps a road sign. Something quick and easy to point the way. What we really ought to have is the Guide Himself. Maps, road signs, a few useful phrases are good things, but infinitely better is Someone who has been there before and knows the way."[7]

In the midst of your busy and stressful day, you may face unexpected situations. Trust God to be our Guide and pray, "Lord, I know this didn't take you by surprise! You knew it was coming and have already made a way for me. I thank You now that You are taking me where I need to go and giving me everything I need to get over the rough spots along the way."

Holy Humor

He who sits in the heavens shall laugh.
Psalm 2:4 NKJV

Is laughter theologically correct? We rarely think of a knee-slapping, rib-tickling, belly laugh when we think of being spiritual. But is that God's perspective?

In Umberto Eco's novel *The Name of the Rose*, a villainous monk named Jorge poisoned anyone who came upon the one book in the monastery library that suggested that God laughed. Jorge feared if the monks thought God laughed, He would become too familiar to them, too common, and they would lose their awe of Him. Jorge probably never considered the idea that laughter is one of the things that sets us apart as made in God's image.

In *Spiritual Fitness*, Doris Donnelly tells us that humor has two elements: an acceptance of life's incongruities and the ability not to take ourselves too seriously. The Christian faith is filled with incongruities — the meek inherit the earth, the simple teach wisdom, death leads to life, a virgin gives birth, a king is born in a stable. Many, but not all of life's incongruities are humorous.[8]

Humor also helps us let go of an exaggerated sense of importance to face the truth about ourselves. Anxiety over our own efforts can obscure what God is doing in our lives. "Lighten up" can be good spiritual advice!

How can we renew our sense of humor?

- Be on the lookout for humor. Almost every situation contains some element of humor.

- Spend time with people who have a sense of humor — their perspective will be contagious.

- Practice laughing. Take a five-to-ten-minute laugh break every day.

You can benefit from laughing. Humor requires a sense of honesty about yourself — without arrogance or false humility. Humor has also been proven to be good for your health. Take time to laugh each day — it is good for the soul as well as the body.

Day By Day

Give us this day our daily bread.
Matthew 6:11 KJV

A mother once stopped by her recently married daughter's home unexpectedly and was promptly greeted with a flood of tears. Alarmed, the mother asked, "What happened, dear?"

Her daughter replied, "It's not what happened, but what keeps happening!"

Even more concerned, the mother asked, "What is it that keeps happening?"

The daughter replied, "Every day there are dishes to be washed. Every day there are meals to be prepared and a lunch to be packed. Every day there is laundry to be done and beds to be made and the house to be cleaned."

"And?" the mother asked, still unsure as to the nature of the problem.

"Don't you see?" the daughter said through her tears. "Life is just so *daily*."

On those days when the "daily-ness" of life seems to have you bogged down in boredom or drudgery, remind yourself the Lord said He would provide for the needs of His people on a daily basis. Manna was gathered in the wilderness every morning. Jesus taught His disciples to pray for their "daily bread." God wants to provide what we need, not only physically and materially, but emotionally and spiritually, one day at a time.

Trust the Lord to give to you:

- the material goods, money, food, and supplies you need today.

- the ideas and creative energy you need for today's work.

- the stamina, health, and strength you need today to fulfill your many roles and responsibilities.

- the spiritual nourishment and fortitude to face and conquer the temptations and trials of today.

The Lord is with you all day, every day, day by day!

Encumbrances

Let us lay aside every weight, and the sin which so easily ensnares us.
Hebrews 12:1 NKJV

In Jules Verne's novel, *The Mysterious Island*, he tells of five men who escape a Civil War prison camp by hijacking a hot-air balloon. As they rise into the air, they realize the wind is carrying them over the ocean. Watching their homeland disappear on the horizon, they wonder how much longer the balloon will stay aloft.

As the hours pass and the surface of the ocean draws closer, the men decide they must cast some of the weight overboard, because they have no way to heat the air in the balloon. Shoes, overcoats, and weapons are reluctantly discarded, and the uncomfortable aviators feel their balloon rise.

However, it isn't long before they find themselves dangerously close to the waves again, so they toss their food overboard. Unfortunately, this too is only a temporary solution and the craft again threatens to lower the men into the sea. One man has an idea: they can tie the ropes that hold the passenger car and sit on them. Then they can cut away the basket beneath them. As they sever do this, the balloon rises again.

Not a minute too soon, they spot land. The five jump into the water and swim to the island. They are alive because they were able to discern the difference between what was really needed and what was not. The "necessities" they once thought they couldn't live without were the very weights that almost cost them their lives.

Why not make an honest assessment of the things that might be slowing you down today? Are they physical or spiritual necessities for you or someone you love? What would your life be like without them? If you eliminated them, would you have more time for the things in your life that really matter?

Ask God to show you how your life could be improved if you made some changes and dropped some things that are weighing you down.

Stop And Think

God...richly furnishes us with everything to enjoy.
1 Timothy 6:17 RSV

It seems that when you're in a hurry and running late you hit nothing but red lights. Although they are annoying when we're racing to an appointment, stop lights are there for our protection.

We need stop lights throughout our day too. Overwork and busy schedules need to be "interrupted" with time for leisure and reflection. Without it we can become seriously sick with stress-induced illnesses. Time set aside for recreation or relaxation can rejuvenate our spirits. This poem by W. H. Davies tells us to take time to "stop and stare":

What is this life if, full of care,
We have no time to stand and stare.
No time to stand beneath the boughs
And stare as long as sheep or cows.

Stop And Think

No time to see, when woods we pass,
Where squirrels hide their nuts in grass.

No time to see, in broad daylight,
Streams full of stars, like stars at night.
No time to turn at Beauty's glance,
And watch her feet, how they can dance.
No time to wait till her mouth can
Enrich that smile her eyes began.
A poor life this if, full of care,
We have no time to stand and stare.[9]

There are two ways of making it through our busy life. One way is to stop thinking. The second is to stop and think. Many people live the first way. They fill every hour with incessant activity. They dare not be alone. There is no time of quiet reflection in their lives. The second way, to stop and think, is to contemplate what life is for and to what end we are living. The word *Sabbath* literally means, "stop doing what you are doing."

Throughout the day today, give yourself a five- or ten-minute "mini-vacation." Get alone, be quiet, and listen for God to speak to you. Make time to be alone with God.

Turning Darkness Into Light

You, O Lord, keep my lamp burning; my God turns my
darkness into light.
Psalm 18:28

It shouldn't take a serious illness to make us stop running around and discover what's really important, but sometimes it does. Sometimes a catastrophe can be a blessing in disguise.

Roger Bone, a physician in Ohio, was diagnosed with renal cancer. Surgeons recommended his right kidney and adrenal gland be removed. After the diagnosis, some of us might have isolated ourselves, become bitter and afraid, or tried to deny that anything serious was wrong. Roger Bone teaches us there's a better approach. He says these four observations have become "a way of life" for him.

1. Good health is often taken for granted; however, it is the most precious commodity one possesses.

2. One's spouse, children, family, and friends are the essential ingredients that allow one to endure an experience such as a serious illness.

3. When faced with death, one realizes the importance of God and one's relationship to God.

4. The things one does throughout life that seem so urgent are, most of the time, not so important.[10]

You can come through the fires of your life with the same positive outlook. Begin today by considering what you value most and hold dearest in life. You may be surprised how your priorities change — and how much richer your life becomes.

A Leather-bound Cover

*For man looketh on the outward appearance, but the Lord
looketh on the heart.*
1 Samuel 16:7 KJV

Dodie Gadient, a schoolteacher for thirteen years, decided to travel across America and see the sights she had taught about. Traveling alone in a truck, with her camper in tow, she launched out. One afternoon in California's rush-hour traffic, the water pump on her truck blew. She was tired, exasperated, and scared that in spite of the traffic jam she caused, no one seemed interested in helping.

Leaning up against the trailer, she finally prayed, "Please God, send me an angel...preferably one with mechanical experience." Within four minutes, a huge Harley drove up, ridden by an enormous man sporting long hair, a beard, and tattooed arms. With an incredible air of confidence, he jumped off and went to work on the truck. A little while later, he flagged down a larger truck, attached a tow chain to the frame of the disabled truck, and whisked the whole 56-foot rig off the freeway onto a side street, where he calmly continued to work on the water pump.

The intimidated schoolteacher was too dumbfounded to talk — especially when she read the paralyzing words on the back of his leather jacket: "Hell's Angels — California." As he finished the task, she finally got up the courage to say, "Thanks so much," and carry on a brief conversation.

Noticing her surprise at the whole ordeal, he looked her straight in the eye and mumbled, "Don't judge a book by its cover. You may not know who you're talking to." With that he smiled, closed the hood of the truck, and straddled his Harley. With a wave, he was gone as fast as he had appeared.[11]

God has a way of opening our eyes, expanding our perspective, and showing us His greatest treasures — people — if we will look beyond our prejudices and preconceived notions. Be open to Him showing you a few of His treasures today!

Playtime!

Unless you change and become like little children,
you will never enter the kingdom of heaven.
Matthew 18:3

A delightful children's poem by Miroslav Holub
gives us a peek into what goes on in a boy's imagination.

A Boy's Head

In it there is a spaceship
and a project for doing away with piano lessons.
And there is Noah's ark
which shall be first.
And there is an entirely new bird,
an entirely new hare,
an entirely new bumble-bee.

There is a river that flows upwards.
There is a multiplication table.
There is anti-matter.

And it just cannot be trimmed.
I believe that only what cannot be trimmed is a head.
There is much promise in the circumstance
that so many people have heads.[12]

Jesus told us we were to *be* like children, not *act* like children! He meant we are to have the unlimited faith and teachability of children. When we are young, everything is new and all situations have the potential for adventure. Even the difficult times are met with a tenacity and courage that we can do whatever is necessary and God will see to it that it will work out fine.

As you take a your break today, let God paint new dreams on your heart. Then have the faith of a child and launch out to make them reality.

God's Promise

*I am with you all the days — perpetually, uniformly,
and on every occasion — to the [very] close
and consummation of the age.*
Matthew 28:20 AMP

A person who conducted an informal survey about the prayers of people in his church found that most people pray one of two types of prayers. The first was an SOS — not only "Save Our Souls," but "Oh God, help us now."

The second was SOP — "Solve our Problems." People asked the Lord to eliminate all needs, struggles, trials, and temptations. They wanted carefree, perfect lives, and fully believed that is what God had promised them. He concluded from his survey: "Most people want God to do it all."

God has not promised, however, to live our lives *for* us — but rather, to walk through our lives *with* us.

God's Promise

Our part is to be faithful and obedient; His part is to lead us, guide us, protect us, and help us. Annie Johnson Flint recognized the true nature of God's promise in this poem:

What God Hath Promised

God hath not promised
Skies always blue,
Flower-strewn pathways
All our lives through;
God hath not promised
Sun without rain,
Joy without sorrow,
Peace without pain.
But God hath promised
Strength for the day,
Rest for the labor,
Light for the way,
Grace for the trials,
Help from above,
Unfailing sympathy,
Undying love.[13]

Do what you know you can do today — and then trust God to do what you *cannot* do!

Knowing Your Worth

But let your yea be yea; and your nay, nay;
lest ye fall into condemnation.
James 5:12 KJV

In his book, *Up from Slavery*, Booker T. Washington describes an ex-slave from Virginia:

"I found that this man had made a contract with his master, two or three years previous to the Emancipation Proclamation, to the effect that the slave was to be permitted to buy himself, by paying so much per year for his body; and while he was paying for himself, he was to be permitted to labor where and for whom he pleased.

"Finding that he could secure better wages in Ohio, he went there. When freedom came, he was still in debt to his master some 300 dollars. Notwithstanding that the Emancipation Proclamation freed him from any obligation to his master, this black man walked the greater portion of *the distance back to where his old master lived in Virginia, and placed the last dollar, with interest, in his hands.*

"In talking to me about this, the man told me that he knew that he did not have to pay his debt, but that he had given his word to his master, and his word he had never broken. He felt that he could not enjoy his freedom till he had fulfilled his promise."[14]

Although he was born into slavery, the man Washington described obviously knew his worth. More important, he knew that as free as a child of God, his word should be trustworthy. He knew he would sleep peacefully if he kept his word to others.

We live in a world where giving our word is not taken seriously. God wants us to walk in blessing and sleep in peace, and that's why He exhorts us to stand by our word.

Be aware of all the times you make promises to people today, and make sure you follow through. Not only will you sleep peacefully, but your friends, family, neighbors, and coworkers will have a new respect for you.

Making It to the Top

*Consider it pure joy, my brothers, whenever you
face trials of many kinds.*

James 1:2

After breaking your back and your ribs, it's very important to regroup. Just ask Jaroslav Rudy, a Czechoslovakian man who has been living in the United States for the past few years.

One day he was riding his motorcycle on a remote trail. While taking a corner a little too fast, he hit a rock and lost control of his bike. Seconds later, he found himself at the bottom of a 30-foot embankment — out of view to anyone who might be riding or walking on the trail.

For two days, Rudy stayed where he'd landed, too injured to move. Freezing temperatures, hunger, and pain finally drove him to try to get back to the trail.

His first attempts were futile — the pain was simply too intense. The next day, beginning at 6 a.m., he tried again. Crawling inch by inch, listening to the sounds of his injured bones crunching, and losing consciousness several times, it took him six hours to reach the trail. That's where four bicyclists spotted him.

A short time later, he was on his way to a hospital.

When your strength is gone and there's a goal you simply must achieve, you don't have to give up, but you do have to be sensible.

- Examine your situation, taking the time to analyze what needs to be done and what resources you have available. Ask the Lord to give you His wisdom and plan.

- Devise a plan of attack, including a timetable for what you hope to accomplish in any given period.

- Take short breaks along the way —to allow your creativity and energy to be renewed.

- Always remember that no matter how much success you achieve, you never really do it alone.

Open the Door!

Behold, I stand at the door and knock; if anyone hears and listens to and heeds My voice and opens the door, I will come in to him and will eat with him, and he [shall eat] with Me.

Revelation 3:20 AMP

A rabbi was visited by a number of learned men one day. He surprised them by asking them this question: "Where is the dwelling of God?"

The men laughed at him, saying, "What a thing to ask! Is not the whole world full of his glory?"

The rabbi answered his own question. "God dwells wherever man lets him in."

We look at the abundance of problems of our world and become overwhelmed by the hunger, disease, abuse, crime, etc. Some of us point to heaven and say, "Where is God? Why doesn't He do something?"

In truth, the Lord is looking at these same situations and crying, "Where are My people? Why don't they do something?"

Perhaps the foremost thing we can do to tackle the problems of our age is this: Invite God into our lives.

When we invite the Lord into our daily lives, we experience His peace and we have a growing understanding of how to live according to His plan. We are transformed by His indwelling Holy Spirit into people who manifest love, care, and morality.

Walking with the Lord every day in this way will cause productivity to flow in your life. He will tell you what problems you are to tackle and how. He will bring people to help you accomplish what He's asked you to do.

Invite God into every place you go today — the shop, factory, business, or school. Ask Him to be a part of every encounter and relationship. He has promised to "come in" to every door that is opened to Him!

Reaching Conclusions

But God chose the foolish things of the world to shame the wise;
God chose the weak things of the world to shame the strong.
1 Corinthians 1:27

Examining life for "deeper meanings" is a common preoccupation and often we draw the wrong conclusions. We assume things are not what they seem, that there is a hidden meaning in what people do when there is none.

Tom Mullen, in *Laughing Out Loud and Other Religious Experiences*, tells about an engineer, a psychologist, and a theologian who were hunting in the wilds of northern Canada. They came across an isolated cabin, and because friendly hospitality is a virtue practiced by those who live in the wilderness, the hunters knocked on the door. When no one answered, they entered the cabin to find two rooms with a minimum of furniture and household equipment. Nothing was unusual about the cabin except the stove, a large, potbellied one made of cast iron — suspended in midair by wires attached to the ceiling beams!

"Fascinating," said the psychologist. "It is obvious that this lonely trapper, isolated from humanity, has elevated his stove so he can curl up under it and vicariously experience a return to the womb." The engineer interrupted, "Nonsense! The man is practicing the laws of thermodynamics. By elevating his stove, he has discovered a way to distribute heat more evenly throughout the cabin."

"With all due respect," said the theologian, "I'm sure that hanging his stove has religious meaning. Fire 'lifted up' has been a religious symbol for centuries." The three debated the point for several minutes and then the trapper returned. When they asked him why he had hung his heavy potbellied stove from the ceiling his answer was succinct: "Had plenty of wire, not much stove pipe!"[15]

Constantly looking for hidden meaning in the actions of coworkers and family members can waste time and create mistrust. Take people at their word today and trust the Lord to bring about His truth in each situation.

Wayside Stops

Jesus...withdrew again to a mountain by himself.
John 6:15

A sanctuary is a place of refuge and protection; a place where you can leave the world behind.

Travelers in the Middle Ages found little shrines set up along the roadway in which a cross and the image of a saint were hung. The traveler could stop at these "sanctuaries" for rest and prayer, regaining strength to continue their journey.

Our contemporary world doesn't have wayside shrines for rest stops. But our minds and hearts still get weary. We have to devise our own wayside stops, not on actual roads, but in the road of daily life.

Attending a worship service on a weekend does not usually provide everything we need to see us through an entire week. As inspiring as the service may be, we need something more to keep us going until the next service. We need stopping places during the week, intimate sanctuaries here and there where we can stop and let God refresh our soul with His presence.

What are some sanctuaries you might find to get away and find restoration?

- Reading Scripture is one such stopping place. Immerse yourself in a favorite passage or psalm.

- A little book of devotion — such as the one you are reading now — is a good way to restore energy.

- A trusted Christian friend with whom you can be yourself is a type of sanctuary. We can gain a great deal from the faith, encouragement, and insight of others.

- Your own communion service during the week gives you a chance to take part in the nourishment of the Lord's Supper.

- Go to a park or sit in your own backyard and read. Or sing aloud a great hymn or praise song.

Jesus is your example, and He often went away to a quiet place to gain strength from His Heavenly Father. Establish your personal shrines today!

What Do You Know?

I consider everything a loss compared to the surpassing greatness of knowing Christ Jesus my Lord.
Philippians 3:8

"Knowledge is of two kinds," said Samuel Johnson. "We know a subject ourselves, or we know where we can find information upon it."

There's also a third area of knowledge: the *unknowable*. Try as we might to uncover all the secrets of the universe, there are simply some things we will never discover or comprehend. As the apostle Paul told the Corinthians, "Now I know in part; then [in the afterlife] I shall know fully, even as I am fully known" (1 Corinthians 13:12).

It's tempting to become a know-it-all. Knowing how to do something, how to fix something, how to find something, gives us a good feeling. We have all experienced the rewards associated with learn-ing new skills and developing them to the best of our ability.

Most of us also enjoy having others turn to us for answers or information. Much of our self-esteem is derived from what we know and what we can do.

But there must be a balance. We must face the hard fact that we can never know everything there is to know about anything. We can never achieve perfection of skill to the point where we never make mistakes. In fact, the more we know about something, the more we realize how much we *don't* know. The more proficient our skills, the more we are aware that accidents happen, some days are "off" days, and everyone has a slump now and then.

If we choose, we can become obsessed with our own perfection and potential, spending all our available time reading and studying and taking courses. We might listen to teaching tapes while we jog and make every vacation "a learning experience."

A wiser approach to life, however, is to spend more time knowing God. The more you know Him, the easier it is to trust Him, hear His voice, and show His love to your family, friends, neighbors, and coworkers. You will learn the things you will need to know in order to do His will. What we know and can do is never as satisfying or meaningful as knowing God and serving others.

Instead of trying to become a "bank of information," become a channel of blessing!

Shortsighted

As we have therefore opportunity, let us do good unto all men,
especially unto them who are of the household of faith.
Galatians 6:10 KJV

Do you miss life-changing opportunities because of shortsightedness? Consider this example:

A fellow approached a cab driver in New York and said, "Take me to London." The cab driver told him there was no possible way for him to drive across the Atlantic. The customer insisted there was. "You'll drive me down to the pier, we'll put the taxi on a freighter to Liverpool, you'll drive me to London, where I'll pay you whatever is on the meter."

The driver agreed, and when they arrived in London, the passenger paid the total on the meter, plus a thousand dollar tip.

The driver roamed around London, not quite knowing what to do. Then an Englishman hailed him and said, "I want you to drive me to New York." The cab driver couldn't believe his good luck. How often can you pick up a fare in London who wants to go to New York?

When the passenger began to say, "First, we take a boat...," the driver cut him off.

"That I know. But where to in New York?"

The passenger said, "Riverside Drive and 104th Street."

The driver responded, "Sorry, I don't go to the west side."

Jesus was well-schooled in the Scriptures, and He often followed the traditions of His heritage. He also had a daily routine of prayer and ministering to the needs of the people. However, He didn't allow traditions or personal preferences to stand in the way of carrying out God's will for the day.

Look for God-given opportunities to serve Him by serving others. Don't allow your daily routines, personal biases, or shortsightedness to miss what the Lord wants to do in you and through you today.

God is Good

Friend, go up higher.
Luke 14:10 KJV

An ancient legend of a swan and a crane tells us about God's goodness — which may be different from what we believe to be good.

A beautiful swan came to rest by the banks of a pond where a crane was wading, seeking snails. For a few minutes the crane looked at the swan and then asked, "Where do you come from?"

The swan replied, "I come from heaven!"

"And where is heaven?" asked the crane.

"Heaven!" replied the swan, "Heaven! have you never heard of heaven?" And the beautiful swan went on to describe the splendor and grandeur of the eternal city. She told the crane about the streets of gold and the gates and walls made of precious stones. She told about the river of life which was as pure as crystal. On the banks of this river stood a tree with leaves for the healing of the nations of the world. In great and eloquent language, the swan described the hosts of saints and angels who lived in the world beyond.

Somewhat surprisingly the crane didn't appear to be the least bit interested in this place the swan described. Eventually he asked the swan, "Are there any snails there?"

"Snails!" declared the swan, obviously revolted at the thought. "No! Of course there are not!"

"Then you can have your heaven," said the crane, as it continued its search along the slimy, muddy banks of the pond, "What I want is snails!"[16]

This fable has a profound truth in it. How many of us turn our backs on the good God has for us in order to search for snails?

Seek out the good that God has for you today. Ask God to give you the desire for *His* good, instead of what *you* consider to be good. Don't bury your head deep in slime when God wants you to experience the delights and joy of His heaven!

Fresh Breezes

I waited patiently and expectantly for the Lord;
and He inclined to me.
Psalm 40:1 AMP

We live our daily lives at such a fast pace, we often don't get beyond the most superficial level. We skim through magazines and books. We channel surf the programs on television. We purchase food in a drive-through and eat it on the way to our next destination. We listen to "sound bites" of opinions on the nightly news, and leave thirty-second phone messages on answering machines. We condense research and opinions into "memo" form.

James Carroll addressed this tendency, writing:

We spend most of our time and energy in a kind of horizontal thinking. We move along the surface of things going from one quick base to another, often with a frenzy that wears us out. We collect data, things, people, ideas "profound experiences," never penetrating any of them.... But there are other times. There are times when we stop. We sit still. We lose ourselves in a pile of leaves or its memory. We listen and breezes from a whole other world begin to whisper.[17]

Perhaps the best thing you can do during your coffee break today is nothing! Shut yourself off from your colleagues. Turn off the ringer on the phone. Stare out the window, and put your mind and heart into neutral.

Communication with God — prayer — is a two-way conversation! It is not just the voicing of praise and petitions, but often *communion*. Sitting in silence with God, listening for whatever He may want to say. Simply enjoy the fact that He is, and you are, and you have a relationship with Him. These special moments with God are when His fresh breezes can enter your heart and refresh you.

Form and Substance

*But when you pray, go into your room, close the door and
pray to your father, who is unseen. Then your Father,
who sees what is done in secret, will reward you.*

Matthew 6:6

America's preoccupation with "image" seems to
have reached outrageous proportions. A Christian, like
everyone else, wants to put his or her best foot forward
as often as possible. Unfortunately, this can sometimes
lead to majoring on form and nearly losing substance
altogether. Consider this story:

A devout Christian who had a cat used to spend
several minutes each day at prayer and meditation in his
bedroom. He read a portion of Scripture and a devotional
book, followed by a period of silent meditation and
prayer. As time went on his prayers became longer and
more intense. He came to cherish this quiet time in his
bedroom, but his cat came to like it too. She would cozy

up to him, purr loudly, and rub her furry body against him. This interrupted the man's prayer time, so he put a collar around the cat's neck and tied her to the bedpost whenever he wanted to be undisturbed while at prayer. This didn't seem to upset the cat, and it meant the man could meditate without interruption.

Over the years, the daughter of this devout Christian had noted how much his devotional time had meant to him. When she began to establish some routines and patterns for her own family, she decided she should do as her father had done. Dutifully, she tied her cat to the bedpost and then proceeded with her devotions. But in her generation time moved faster and she couldn't spend as much time at prayer as her father did.

The day came when her son was grown up. He also wanted to preserve some of the family tradition which had meant so much to his mother and his grandfather. But the pace of life had quickened all the more and there simply was no time for elaborate devotional proceedings. So he eliminated the time for meditation, Bible reading, and prayer. But in order to carry on the tradition, each day while he was dressing, he tied the family cat to the bedpost!

Window on the World

O Lord, I pray, open his eyes that he may see.
2 Kings 6:17 NASB

A story from England called "The Wonderful Window" tells about a London clerk who worked in drab and depressing circumstances. His office building was in a rundown part of the city and had not been maintained.

But that ordinary clerk was not about to let his outlook on life be determined by the dreariness of his surroundings. So one day he bought a beautiful, multi-colored Oriental window painted with an inspiring scene.

The clerk took his window to his workplace and had it installed high up on the wall in his office. When the hardworking, dispirited clerk looked through his window, he did not see the familiar slum scenes, with dark streets and dirty marketplaces. Instead he saw a fairy city with beautiful castles and towers, green parks, and lovely homes on wide tree-lined streets. On the highest tower of the window there was a large white banner with a strong knight protecting the fair city from a fierce and dangerous dragon. This wonderful window put a "halo" on the everyday tasks of the young man.

Somehow as he worked long hours at tedious book work and accounting, trying to make everything balance, he felt he was working for that knight on the banner. This feeling produced a sense of honor and dignity. He had found a noble purpose helping the knight keep the city happy, beautiful, prosperous, and strong.

You don't have to let your circumstances or surroundings discourage you, either. God has sent you to your place of work — whether it is at home, in an office, at a school, or in a factory — to do noble work for Him. You His worker, bringing His beauty to everyone around you.

Stay In the Game

To him who overcomes, I will give the right to sit with me on my throne, just as I overcame and sat down with my Father on his throne.
Revelation 3:21

You don't have to be a chess player to appreciate what happened in Philadelphia on February 17, 1996. Man defeated computer in an internationally-observed classical chess match.

Garry Kasparov, world chess champ, didn't win quite so easily as he had hoped to. He lost the first of the six games to Deep Blue, the IBM super-computer. It was just what he needed, however, because it forced him to pay even closer attention, devise more intricate strategies, and learn more about a sport in which he is an acknowledged expert.

Kasparov notched three wins of his own and two draws in the remaining five games of the week-long match. It took every bit of chess knowledge he possessed — and some he developed along the way — to defeat a computer that is capable of calculating fifty billion positions in just three minutes.

When you have to face a "challenger" who seems to outweigh you, what can you do?

1. Have confidence in your own abilities, but don't get cocky.

2. If possible, prepare beforehand. That means study and practice.

3. Do a test run, with simulated "game" conditions (for example, give the speech or read the report in front of a family audience).

4. During your warm-ups, take short breaks. Use them to evaluate how you're doing or just to give your mind a rest.

5. Pray!

On "game day," relax. Let all the information you've stored in your brain rise to the top. Expect the unexpected and be ready to improvise and make midcourse adjustments as needed. And, save a little something for the next game!

The Trouble with Being Right

*Take heed to yourselves: If thy brother trespass against thee,
rebuke him; and if he repent, forgive him.*
Luke 17:3 KJV

Believe it or not, it's often harder to gracefully receive an apology than it is to issue one. As Christians, we know we are to forgive "seventy times seven" times (Matthew 18:22 KJV), but some of us can sincerely forgive and still project an air of superiority unbecoming to a child of the King.

If you're waiting for someone to realize they owe you an apology, use your coffee break to think of a response that reflects genuine forgiveness and allows the transgressor to feel he has retained your respect. Consider this humorous little story:

A passenger on a dining car looked over the luncheon menu. The list included both a chicken salad sandwich and a chicken sandwich. He decided on the chicken salad sandwich, but absentmindedly wrote chicken sandwich on the order slip. When the waiter brought the chicken sandwich the customer angrily protested.

Most waiters would have immediately picked up the order slip and shown the customer the mistake was his. This waiter didn't. Instead, expressing regret at the error, he picked up the chicken sandwich, returned to the kitchen, and a moment later placed a chicken salad sandwich in front of the customer.

While eating his sandwich, the customer picked up the order slip and saw that the mistake was his. When it came time to pay the check the man apologized to the waiter and offered to pay for both sandwiches. The waiter's response was, "No, sir. That's perfectly all right. I'm just happy you've forgiven me for being right."

By taking the blame initially and allowing the passenger to discover his own mistake, the waiter accomplished several things: he allowed the passenger to retain his dignity, reminded him to be more cautious before blaming others, and created a better atmosphere for everyone in the dining car. Next time someone blames you for their mistake, don't get defensive, but find a creative way to make things right.

Worry Is a Rat

Who of you by worrying can add a single hour to his life?
Luke 12:25

In the middle of the morning, in the middle of the night, even when you don't think you are thinking about it — there it is — that thing you've been worrying about. Worry is a destructive force that never helps solve problems, but adds stress and often hinders finding solutions. Worry is not intended to be a part of God's plan for your life!

In his book, *Questions Jesus Asked*, Dr. Clovis Chappell gives this example:

"Years ago, in the pioneer days of aviation, a pilot was making a flight around the world. After he had been gone for some two hours from his last landing field, he heard a noise in his plane which he recognized as the gnawing of a rat. For all he knew the rat could be gnawing through a vital cable or control of the plane. It was a very serious

situation. He was both concerned and anxious. At first he did not know what to do. It was two hours back to the landing field from which he had taken off and more than two hours to the next field ahead.

"Then he remembered that the rat is a rodent. It is not made for the heights; it is made to live on the ground and under the ground. Therefore the pilot began to climb. He went up a thousand feet, then another thousand and another until he was more than twenty thousand feet up. The gnawing ceased. The rat was dead. He could not survive in the atmosphere of those heights. More than two hours later the pilot brought the plane safely to the next landing field and found the dead rat.

"Brothers and sisters in Christ, worry is a rodent. It cannot live in the secret place of the Most High. It cannot breathe in the atmosphere made vital by prayer and familiarity with the Scripture. Worry dies when we ascend to the Lord through prayer and His Word."[18]

Prayer Pause

Uphold me according to Your promise, that I may live.
Psalm 119:116 AMP

A coffee break is a good time for prayer!

When we pray at the outset of our day, our prayer is often for general guidance and help from the Lord. When we pray in the midst of our day, our prayer is much more likely to be specific and aimed at immediate needs and concerns. By the time a coffee break rolls around, we have a much better idea of what our day holds, including what particular dangers, difficulties, or temptations we are going to face! It is with that knowledge born of experience that this prayer of St. Patrick takes on even greater meaning:

*M*ay the wisdom of God instruct me,
the eye of God watch over me,
the ear of God hear me,

the word of God give me sweet talk,
the hand of God defend me,
the way of God guide me.

Christ be with me.
Christ before me.
Christ in me.
Christ under me.
Christ over me.
Christ on my right hand.
Christ on my left hand.
Christ on this side.
Christ on that side.
Christ in the head of everyone to whom I speak.
Christ in the mouth of every person who speaks to me.
Christ in the eye of every person who looks upon me.
Christ in the ear of everyone who hears me today.
Amen.[19]

Take time in the middle of your day to ask the Lord for His wrap-around presence, His unending encouragement, and His all-sustaining assistance. And be a vessel that carries His presence, encouragement, and assistance to others.

One Another

Love one another.
1 John 4:7 NASB

The Bible has much to say about how we are to relate to other people. On your break, meditate on the Scripture verses below and then ask God to help you show others the love He has for them.

- Bear *one another's* burdens and, thus fulfill the law of Christ (Galatians 6:2).

- Be subject to *one another* (Ephesians 5:21).

- Comfort *one another* (1 Thessalonians 4:18).

- Stir *one another* up to love and good works — encouraging *one another* (Hebrews 10:24-25).

- Be hospitable to *one another* (1 Peter 4:9).

- Employ God's gifts for *one another* (1 Peter 4:10).

- Confess your faults to *one another* and be healed (James 5:16).

* Live in harmony with *one another* (Romans 12:16, 15:5; Colossians 3:15).
* Do not judge *one another* (Romans 14:13).
* Build *one another* up (Romans 14:19; 1 Thessalonians 3:12-13; Ephesians 4:15-16).
* Accept *one another* (Romans 15:7).
* Instruct and admonish *one another* (Romans 15:14; Colossians 3:16).
* Serve *one another* (Galatians 5:13; John 13:14).
* Forbear *one another* (Ephesians 4:2; Colossians 3:13).
* Speak the truth to *one another* (Ephesians 4:25).
* Be kind to *one another* (Ephesians 4:32).
* Forgive *one another* (Ephesians 4:32; Colossians 3:13).

"Almighty God, you have so linked our lives one with another that all we do affects, for good or ill, all other lives: so guide us in the work we do, that we may do it not for self alone, but for the common good; and, as we seek a proper return for our own labour, make us mindful of the rightful aspirations of other workers, and arouse our concern for those who are out of work; through Jesus Christ our Lord, who lives and reigns with you and the Holy Spirit, one God, for ever and ever." — Unknown.[20]

Can-Do Attitude

And Jesus said unto him, No man, having put his hand to the
plow, and looking back, is fit for the kingdom of God.
Luke 9:62 KJV

Walter E. Isenhour wrote a clever poem that appeared in *The Wesleyan Youth* many years ago. Originally written for teens, its message is, nonetheless, timeless and for all ages and circumstances.

Watch Your Can't's and Can's

If you would have some worthwhile plans
You've got to watch your can't's and can's;
You can't aim low and then rise high;
You can't succeed if you don't try;
You can't go wrong and come out right;
You can't love sin and walk in the light;
You can't throw time and means away
And live sublime from day to day.

Can-Do Attitude

You can be great if you'll be good
And do God's will as all men should;
You can ascend life's upward road,

Although you bear a heavy load;
You can be honest, truthful, clean,
By turning from the low and mean;
You can uplift the souls of men
By words and deeds, or by your pen.
So watch your can't and watch your can's.
And watch your walks and watch your stands,
And watch the way you talk and act,
And do not take the false for fact;
And watch the things that mar or make;
For life is great to every man
Who lives to do the best he can.[21]

As your day progresses, keep in mind that your life goes in the direction you aim it. A popular saying in recent years sums up this idea succinctly: "Whether you think you can, or can't...you're right." Have an "I can" attitude today, and then pursue excellence with all your ability.

Stay Involved

Trust in the Lord and do good.
Psalm 37:3 KJV

*Y*ou know it's a bad day when...your twin sister forgets your birthday. Your income tax refund check bounces. You put both contact lenses in the same eye. You wake up in traction in the hospital and your insurance agent says your accident policy covers falling off the roof, but not hitting the ground.

How do we recover from those times when everything seems to go wrong? How do we cope when things seem to go from bad to worse?

The temptation during those times is to focus on ourselves and on the problems that seem to be relentless. But the best thing to do is just the opposite — get involved with other people.

Comedian George Burns said the key to happiness is helping others: "If you were to go around asking people what would make them happier, you'd get answers like a new car, a bigger house, a raise in pay, winning a lottery, a face-lift, more kids, less kids, a new restaurant to go to — probably not one in a hundred would say a chance to help people. And yet that may bring the most happiness of all.

"I don't know Dr. Jonas Salk, but after what he's done for us with his polio vaccine, if he isn't happy, he should have that brilliant head of his examined. Of course, not all of us can do what he did. I know I can't do what he did; he beat me to it.

"But the point is, it doesn't have to be anything that extraordinary. It can be working for a worthy cause, performing a needed service, or just doing something that helps another person."[22]

What are some ways to help others? A smile or an unexpected courtesy to a stressed coworker. A thank-you note or card to let a distant friend know you are thinking of them. A bouquet of flowers for the secretary for no special reason except to let her know she is appreciated. Be imaginative and creative in your deeds of kindness. On those bad days when nothing seems to go right...*you* can contribute something "right!"

God Knows!

Even the very hairs of your head are all numbered.
Matthew 10:30 AMP

Do you ever wonder if God has lost your address? Perhaps He has lost track of you or even forgotten you? God's Word answers that thought with a resounding, "Not so!"

Jesus taught His followers, "Are not two little sparrows sold for a penny? And yet not one of them will fall to the ground without your Father's leave [consent] and notice....Fear not, then; you are of more value than many sparrows" (Matthew 10:29, 31 AMP).

The psalmist also recognized God's thorough and intimate knowledge of us. Read these words from Psalm 139 and be encouraged. The Lord not only knows *you*, but He knows precisely what you are facing and experiencing today. Even if you are not *aware* of His presence, you can rest assured He is by your side:

God Knows!

"O Lord, you have examined my heart and know everything about me. You know when I sit or stand. When far away you know my every thought. You chart the path ahead of me, and tell me where to stop and rest. Every moment, you know where I am. You know what I am going to say before I even say it. You both precede and follow me, and place your hand of blessing on my head.

This is too glorious, too wonderful...I can never be lost to your Spirit! I can never get away from my God!...

You saw me before I was born and scheduled each day of my life before I began to breathe. Every day was recorded in your Book!

How precious it is, Lord, to realize that you are thinking about me constantly! I can't even count how many times a day your thoughts turn towards me. And when I waken in the morning, you are still thinking of me!"

Psalm 139:1-7,16-18
The Living Bible

Accepting Substitutes

Now unto him that is able to do exceeding abundantly above all that we ask or think, according to the power that worketh in us.
Ephesians 3:20 KJV

A recently married woman moved to a small town in Wyoming. Clothing stores were in short supply and her busy ranch life left little time for the long trips to larger cities to shop. Her situation was made more difficult by the fact that she was a hard-to-fit size. To solve her problem, she began relying on a major store catalog which carried her size. The printed order forms sent by the store had this sentence at the bottom: "If we do not have the article you ordered in stock, may we substitute?"

Since she rarely ordered unless she really needed the article in question, she was hesitant to trust strangers to make an appropriate substitution, but she replied "yes," hoping it wouldn't be necessary.

This approach worked well until one day she opened a package from the company and found a letter which read, in part, "We are sorry that the article you ordered is out of stock, but we have substituted…" When she unwrapped the merchandise she found an article of greater quality worth double the price she paid!

On each order after that, the woman wrote "YES" in large red letters at the bottom of the order form by the substitution question. She had confidence the store would provide her with the best they had to fill her order.

When we pray to God, we are wise to add to our requests that we are quite willing to accept a substitution for what we think we need. We can trust God to send us the perfect answer because, as our Maker, He knows what will fit us better than we do. Because He knows the future in a way that we do not, He can answer in a way that goes beyond our highest expectations. Every time He sends "substitutes," we can be sure He is sending something much better than we could have ever imagined.

Whose Strength?

When I am weak, then I am strong.
2 Corinthians 12:10 NKJV

In the springtime it's fun to watch tiny baby birds with downy crowns begin to find their way around. They make their way to the edge of their nest and take a peek over to view the very large, unexplored world around them.

At first they may look into the abyss and then shrink back to the familiar security of their nest. Perhaps they imagine the strength of their own untried wings is all that will save them from a fatal fall — and they know how weak and unproven those little wings are! Yet, when they are either pushed out of the nest or gather courage to launch out on their own to try that first flight, they find the air supports them when they spread their wings.

How often do we allow unfamiliar situations and circumstances to loom large and threatening in our imagination? Sometimes when we look at circumstances that lie outside our familiar "nest" we may feel just like a baby bird. We take a look at our own weakness and we may want to turn around and head back to safety.

In times of crisis — either real or imagined — what is it that God has called us to do? He may be trying to push us out of our nest and "stretch our wings," so we can grow in our faith.

When Peter saw the Lord Jesus walking on the Sea of Galilee, he cried out, "Lord, if it's you, tell me to come to you on the water." Jesus replied, "Come." Peter got out of the boat and walked on the water toward Jesus. It was when he took his eyes off Jesus and focused on the wind that he became frightened and began to sink. He cried out, "Lord, save me!" And, of course, Jesus did!

When you look to your own resources you may get a "sinking" feeling. This morning, look to Jesus and His resources. Then you will have courage to venture into unknown territory!

What Nature?

*The Lord is my Shepherd [to feed, guide, and shield me]; I shall
not lack....only goodness, mercy, and unfailing love shall follow
me all the days of my life.*
Psalm 23:1,6 AMP

How do you picture God? Many people see
Him as a stern judge, just waiting to pounce on those
who break His laws. Others see Him as the Supreme
Power of the universe, distant and remote, uninvolved
in their lives. Still others have come to enjoy a loving,
intimate relationship with their Heavenly Father.

Danish theologian Sören Kierkegaard provides a
wonderful word picture in this prayer:

"*Father in Heaven, when the thought of thee wakes in
our hearts, let it not awaken like a frightened bird that flies
about in dismay, but like a child waking from its sleep with
a heavenly smile.*"

What Nature?

How we regard God has a direct impact on how we pray, as well as how we treat others. If we see God as a stern Judge, we tend to be more judgmental and less forgiving, even to ourselves. Our prayers, if we are brave enough to pray them, tend to be focused on requests for forgiveness and petitions for retribution on our enemies.

If we see God as distant and remote, we are likely to dismiss Him from our lives completely, turning to others for love and acceptance. Ultimately, we become frustrated, because no one can give us the unconditional love God can.

However, if we believe in God as our loving, generous Heavenly Father, we are much more likely to communicate with Him about *everything*. We are also more willing to communicate with others and forgive them for their frailties and faults.

In the end, every aspect of our lives, including work, is impacted by the nature of our relationship with God.

How *do* you regard Him?

Who's Watching?

That ye would walk worthy of God,
who hath called you unto his kingdom and glory.
1 Thessalonians 2:12 KJV

Even though we are Christians, we have to live our lives and conduct our business like everyone else, right? After all, we are only human!

Wrong! Once we have accepted Jesus into our lives, we have the supernatural power of the Holy Spirit to help us be and do more than what is humanly possible. Even nonbelievers know that people who call themselves followers of Christ should operate differently than those who don't.

Take, for instance, this account of a man named Roy. He had been a kidnapper and holdup man for twelve years, but while in prison he heard the Gospel and invited Jesus Christ into his life: "Jesus said to me, 'I will come and live in you and we will serve this sentence together.' And we did."

Several years later he was paroled, and just before he went out he was handed a two-page letter written by another prisoner, which said, "You know perfectly well that when I came into the jail I despised preachers, the Bible, and anything that smacked of Christianity. I went to the Bible class and the preaching service because there wasn't anything else interesting to do.

"Then they told me you were saved, and I said, 'There's another fellow taking the Gospel road to get parole.' But, Roy, I've been watching you for two-and-a-half years. You didn't know it, but I watched you when you were in the yard exercising, when you were working in the shop, when you played, while we were all together at meals, on the way to our cells, and all over, and now I'm a Christian, too, because I watched you. The Saviour [sic] who saved you has saved me. You never made a slip."

Roy says, "When I got that letter and read it, through, I broke out in a cold sweat. Think of what it would have meant if I had slipped, even once."[23]

Who might be secretly watching you? A coworker, a child, a boss, or a spouse who needs to know Jesus? You are His representative to that person.

On Call

O that I had wings like a dove!
I would fly away and be at rest.
Psalm 55:6 RSV

𝒫orch swings, picnic tables, and handwritten letters almost seem like relics of a bygone age. Symbols of today's fast-paced culture are fast-food drive-throughs, computer games, and e-mail. In spite of the changes in our cultural icons, we actually may not be that much busier than the last generation — after all, we still only have 24 hours in a day.

The problem is, however, that we seldom "get away from it all." Experts say that communication technology gives immediate access to anyone, virtually anywhere. We are no more than a beeper or a cellular phone-call away from being summoned.

Because of that phenomenon, Dr. Mark Moskowitz of Boston University's Medical Center observes, "A lot of people are working 24 hours a day, seven days a week, even when they're not technically at work." That is a precursor to first-class exhaustion.

Government executive Roy Neel quit his job as deputy chief of staff in the Clinton Administration and took a slower-paced job. He realized that work "even for the President of the United States" was not worth the price. It hit home for Roy the night he and his 9-year-old son Walter were ready to walk out the door for a long promised baseball game. The phone rang, and it was the President. Walter was not impressed with a call from the White House. What he wanted was to go to a baseball game with his dad. After the hour-long phone call, Roy discovered his son had found a ride to the game with a neighbor. He commented, "Our society has become schizophrenic. We praise people who want balance in their lives, but reward those who work themselves to death."[24]

When asked his formula for success, physicist Albert Einstein spelled it out this way: "If A is success in life, then A equals x plus y plus z. Work is x, y is play, and z is keeping your mouth shut." What a genius!

Knowing God's Will

Now therefore, I pray You, if I have found favor in Your sight,
show me now Your way.
Exodus 33:13 AMP

"*K*nowing the will of God" — both the big picture and the daily details — concerns every Christian. We all need to ask often, *What is it God wants me to do? How is it He wants me to live?*

St. Ignatius of Loyola saw the doing of God's will as not only our command in life, but also our reward:

"*T*each us, good Lord, to serve thee as thou deservest:
to give and not to count the cost; to fight and not to heed
the wounds; to toil and not to seek for rest; to labor and
not to ask for any reward save that of knowing that we
do thy will."[25]

It is as we know we are doing God's will that we find true meaning in life and a deep sense of accomplishment and purpose.

Knowing God's Will

How can we know that we are doing God's will? One of the simplest approaches is this:

First, commit yourself to the Lord each day, and periodically throughout the day, by simply saying, "Lord, I put my life in Your hands. Do with me what You will."

Second, trust the Lord to send you the work and the relationships you need for His purpose in your life to be accomplished.

As Roberta Hromas, a noted Bible teacher, once said: "Simply answer your door, answer your phone, and answer your mail. The Lord will put in your path the opportunities that He desires for you to pursue."

God's will is not a mystery you try desperately to unlock. He does not desire His will to be a secret, because the Bible is filled with scriptures about knowing His will. The key is to see His will, to listen to the Holy Spirit and read and study His Word. Then you can know what He has planned for you!

A Quiet Moment

*For thus saith the Lord God, the Holy One of Israel; In
returning and rest shall ye be saved; in quietness and in
confidence shall be your strength.*
Isaiah 30:15 KJV

Between the great issues of life there is quiet.
Silence characterizes the highest in art and the deepest
in nature. It's the silence between the notes that give
them rhythm, interest, and emphasis.

The surest spiritual search is made in silence.
Moses learned in Midian and Paul in Arabia what
would have eluded them in the noisy streets of men.

Silence reaches beyond words. The highest point
in drama is silence. The strongest of emotions don't
always cry aloud. The most effective reproof is not a
tongue lashing. The sincerest sympathy is not wordy or
noisy. The best preparation for an emergency is the
calm of quietness.

A Quiet Moment

Time spent in quiet prayer is the best preparation for intelligent action. The best proof of quality is often silence; the great engine is almost noiseless. The best indicator of confidence is almost always silence. The person who is confident of their position does not argue or raise their voice or even try to explain everything.

Quiet times are most cherished in the middle of busy days. Sometimes the quiet does not offer itself; it must be sought out. At other times, the surroundings don't allow for true silence. It is in those moments when the Holy Spirit can supernaturally turn down the volume and allow moments of quiet communion with God from within.

A coffee break is a perfect time to seek a quiet spot for a few minutes of real refreshment in the presence of a "still, small voice" (1 Kings 19:12 KJV).

Praise Break

Oh, give thanks to the Lord, for he is good;
his lovingkindness continues forever.
Psalm 136:1 TLB

Rather than take a coffee break today, take a praise break!

Take a pause in your day to acknowledge all the ways in which the Lord has been good to you — not in general, but be specific. Thank Him for what He is doing in your life, right now, where you are.

Nothing is too large or too small to be worthy of your praise. Every good thing you have and experience in life ultimately comes from the Lord. Sometimes blessings come directly and sometimes through the talents or skills of others who are inspired or empowered by Him. Give praise for the things you see at hand!

Praise Break

Your praise list may include:
- help with writing that important memo
- a good, kind, and thorough secretary
- the invention of paper clips and staplers
- a window through which to view the world
- vacuum cleaners
- microwave ovens
- walking shoes
- trees that are starting to bud
- ready access to vital data
- computer repairmen
- an unfailing copy machine
- the postman being five minutes late, which gave you time to find a stamp
- a cordial interview
- willing colleagues
- doormats, and children who remember to use them
- a cake that survived a slammed back door
- a completed phone call
- spell-check
- good health
- fulfilling work
- a loving family and circle of friends

Look around, look down, look up. You'll never run out of things to be thankful for!

Take Cover

He will cover you with His pinions,
and under His wings you may seek refuge.
His faithfulness is a shield and bulwark.
Psalm 91:4 NASB

*B*ouncing back from disappointment, loss, or an irritating situation can take time. When you're hurting, the thing you need to do is nurse your wounds for a little while, regroup, then go back out and face the world.

Wouldn't it be nice if that saying we learned as children was true in our lives today — "I'm rubber, you're glue. Everything you say bounces off me and sticks to you"? What a relief it would be if angry words, dirty looks, and cruel actions had no power to hurt us.

Many of us have frying pans coated with Teflon, because food doesn't stick to it. The scientists at Dow Chemical have come up with what might be called the next generation of Teflon: a fluorocarbon formula that can be sprayed or brushed onto a surface. It's been suggested it might be used to repel graffiti on subway walls, to ward off barnacles on ships, dirt on wallpaper, and ice on aircraft. This substance is actually an adhesive and an abhesive. Its "base" sticks to whatever it's applied to, but its "surface" repels moisture.

This is a little like being in the world, but not of it. "I pray not that thou shouldest take them out of the world, but that thou shouldest keep them from the evil," Jesus prayed for His disciples in John 17:15-16 (KJV). "As thou has sent me into the world, even so have I also sent them into the world" (v. 18).

We have to come into contact with a lot of negatives throughout our lives, but we don't have to absorb them or let them become part of us. With the help of the Holy Spirit, we can stick to God. Then His presence and power in our lives will not allow us to be coated with anything that will drag us down.

Coffee Break with God

Administrivia

*Let us strip off anything that slows us down or holds us back,
and especially those sins that wrap themselves
so tightly around our feet and trip us up.*
Hebrews 12:1 TLB

A university provost once moaned to a fellow administrator, "Today has not been the best of days."

"What happened?" his colleague asked.

He explained, "Nothing major. I just got bogged down in the mire of administrivia."

Some days are like that. We find ourselves swallowed up by small but necessary routine chores. Administrative tasks are generally performed for the good of the family, organization, or institution, but rarely with a sense of personal satisfaction.

Henry David Thoreau offered this advice for those who seem to be swallowed up by the mundane:

❀ · ❀ · ❀ · ❀ · ❀ · ❀ · ❀ · ❀ · ❀ · ❀ · ❀ · ❀

"*Our life is frittered away by detail.... I say, let your affairs be as two or three, and not a hundred or a thousand; instead of a million count half a dozen, and keep your accounts on your thumbnail.... Simplify, simplify. Instead of three meals a day, if it be necessary eat but one; instead of a hundred dishes, five; and reduce other things in proportion.*

"*Let us spend every day as deliberately as Nature, and not be thrown off the track by every nutshell and mosquito's wing that falls on the rails.*"[26]

We may not be able to reduce all our tasks or obligations to "two or three" a day, but what we can do is make sure each day includes two or three things that are meaningful. Our accomplishment of those things will make the mundane or difficult chores more tolerable, and give us a great deal of satisfaction in the end.

A Kite's Tale

Just as each of us has one body with many members, and these
members do not all have the same function.
Romans 12:4

During the Sunday "children's sermon," a pastor gathered the little ones around him and told this story:

On a breezy March day, the town mayor happened through the park where a small boy was flying the largest, most beautiful kite he had ever seen. It soared so high and floated so gently, the mayor was sure it must be visible from the next town. Since his little town did not have very many things of note to its credit, the mayor decided to award a "key to the city" to the one responsible for setting this spectacle aloft.

"Who is responsible for flying this kite?" the mayor inquired.

"I am," said the boy. "I made the kite with my own hands. I painted all the beautiful pictures and constructed it with scraps I found in my father's workshop. I fly the kite," he declared.

"I am," said the wind. "It is my whim that keeps it aloft and sets the direction it will go. Unless I blow, the kite will not fly at all. I fly the kite," the wind cooed.

"Not so," exclaimed the kite's tail. "I make it sail and give it stability against the wind's whims. Without me, the kite would spin out of control and not even the boy could save it from crashing to earth. I fly the kite," declared the tail.

Now who flies the kite? — the pastor asked.

"They all do!" said several kids in concert. Smart kids!

Sometimes adults aren't so smart. In the hurry of a business day, its easy to forget that the boss or team leader is just that, the leader of the team. Each member is important in keeping projects moving and meeting goals.

Take a moment to consider your coworkers. Ask yourself, "How would our progress be changed if that person's job didn't exist?" Next time you pass their work area, tell them you're glad they are part of the team!

Unchanging Hope

He will not fear evil tidings;
his heart is steadfast, trusting in the Lord.
Psalm 112:7 NASB

No one knows for sure when ships were first used for water transportation. The earliest evidence of sailing vessels dates from Egypt about the third millennium b.c. Since then ships have changed considerably.

Today's passenger and cargo ships have no oars, sails, or masts. Modern vessels have all the conveniences of a great luxury hotel — gourmet cuisine, an array of entertainment, recreation, even swimming pools! One thing, however, has remained remarkably the same — the anchor. Except for the differing sizes, the anchor on Paul's ship of the first century and the anchor on the *Queen Elizabeth II* of the 20th century are not much different.

The same could be said of human life. Technology has brought staggering changes in virtually every arena of our lives. However people are still people. We experience the same struggles, temptations, joys, hopes, and sorrows of our ancestors — and our souls still need an anchor.

When Paul and his companions were shipwrecked on the coast of Malta, they dropped four anchors, which kept the ship from being dashed against the rocks. The writer of Hebrews tells us we have an anchor that will keep our lives from shipwreck — our hope in Jesus Christ.

Jesus keeps us safe and secure in the midst of storms and uncertainties. No matter what we face, because He is Lord of our lives, we have hope...hope for the future, hope to be healed, hope to succeed, hope to be free, hope to help others.

Just as no experienced sailor would go out to sea without an anchor, we must never go anywhere without Jesus![27]

Good, Better, Best

I have set before you life and death, blessings and curses.
Now choose life, so that you and your children may live
and that you may love the Lord your God, listen to his voice,
and hold fast to him. For the Lord is your life.
Deuteronomy 30:19-20

As children, we can't wait to grow up and finish school. In our twenties, we scramble for a job and try to decide which career is the best fit. In our thirties, we struggle to balance home and work.

In our forties, some of us face the empty nest and use the time to rediscover old passions or find new activities to challenge us. In our fifties, we make a last push to prepare for inevitable retirement. Movement, movement, movement.

Then, one day, the daily grind comes to an abrupt halt and we have a choice to make: Vegetate or keep moving.

If we're fortunate like Richard Wesley Hamming, we don't have to wonder how we'll fill the time. In the late 1940s, Hamming wrote the codes known as the Hamming Codes. They enable computers to correct their own mistakes. For the last twenty years he has been "educating admirals" in computer science at a Navy school.

Hamming, now 81, admits the older he gets, the harder it is to stay enthused — but he's not quitting and neither should you!

We can't always depend on others to inspire us, so how do we maintain our zest for living? Ask yourself this: Will it be difficult to stay inspired in heaven? Not a chance! There is no sickness, unlimited energy, and an environment of peace, love, and joy. The good news is, Jesus told us we don't have to wait for the kingdom of heaven; it's inside of us. (See Luke 17:20-21.)

Today, when things get tough, look within and bring some heaven to earth!

The Jordan

Behold, a King will reign in righteousness, and princes will rule
in justice. And each one of them shall be like...
streams of water in a dry place.
Isaiah 32:1-2 AMP

The Jordan River is one of the foremost landmarks in the Middle East. It is mentioned in the Bible nearly 200 times.

There are three interesting facts about the Jordan River that relate to our lives in a spiritual way. First, the river covers an area of about 65 miles from the Sea of Galilee to the Dead Sea, but the river itself winds back and forth so often it is actually almost 200 miles long! Rarely in our lives do we have a "straight shot" from failure to success, but many twists and turns along the way.

Second, the river drops significantly in altitude — more than 600 feet, which produces numerous rapids along the normally calm river. The same is true for us. We move at a steady pace, but every now and then we have a growth spurt and hit some fast currents.

Third, the Scriptures tell us of many miracles that happened in or by the Jordan River. A heavy ax head floated on its surface, the children of Israel crossed it the same way they crossed the Red Sea, Naaman was cured of leprosy by dipping in it seven times, Elijah was taken to heaven just after crossing it, and Jesus was baptized in it.

However, what the Jordan has done for thousands of years is provide life-giving water to people, livestock, and farms along its banks. Its waters have made the Jordan River Valley one of the most fruitful in the world. This is the daily miracle of the Jordan.

As you experience changes of pace and direction, along with a miracle now and then, remember your daily miracle — bringing God's life-giving Water, the Gospel of His Son, Jesus Christ, to those around you.

What a Friend!

I have called you friends.
John 15:15 RSV

What a friend we have in Jesus,
All our sins and griefs to bear!
What a privilege to carry
Everything to God in prayer!
O what peace we often forfeit!
O what needless pain we bear!
All because we do not carry
Everything to God in prayer.

Joseph Scriven, the writer of the hymn "What a Friend We Have in Jesus," had a life of great sorrow. A day or two before their wedding, his fiancee drowned. This tragedy put him in a melancholy state that stayed with him the rest of his life.

In spite of his despondent temperament, the power and presence of God were evident in Scriven's life. He was a philanthropist and a devout Christian. He had a reputation as the man "who saws wood for poor widows and sick people who are unable to pay." To other people Scriven *was* the friend that they had found in Jesus.

Scriven wrote this hymn to comfort his mother in a time of sorrow. He never intended that anyone else would see it, but the manuscript was discovered by a neighbor. When asked if he had written it, Scriven said, "The Lord and I did it between us."[28]

Spend your break today with your best friend, Jesus. He didn't die for you so you could go through struggles alone and carry heavy burdens by yourself. He gave Himself so you and He could become friends, and friends always stand by and help each other.

You only need to share your need with the Lord Jesus in prayer to find comfort!

Whatsoever Things Are Just

*Woe to those who enact evil statutes, and to those who
constantly record unjust decisions, so as to deprive the needy of
justice, and rob the poor of My people of their rights.*
Isaiah 10:1-2 NASB

It's satisfying to have a career that puts our brain to the test and utilizes our creativity. Even better is having a "mission" in life that gives us the opportunity to minister to others.

George F. R. Ellis is a well-known cosmologist. On his "day job," he evaluates and devises theories concerning the origin and structure of the universe. His "calling," however, is to identify and eliminate injustice where he finds it.

Growing up in Johannesburg, South Africa, Ellis observed plenty of injustice. His father lost his newspaper job for criticizing the government. His mother helped found a group of white women voters who spent forty years fighting apartheid.

After Ellis left home to study at the University of Cambridge, he joined the Society of Friends (Quakers) and embraced their rational, nonviolent ways. He returned to South Africa to teach, and do all he could do to bring an end to apartheid.

Ellis first helped raise money to set up an orphanage and a program to distribute milk. He devised a basic housing plan for the needy, which was initially rejected by the government, but later adopted.

Next he gathered and publicized evidence about the government's "undeclared war" against blacks. He didn't win any popularity contests for that effort. Many whites in South Africa thought Ellis was crazy to put his neck on the line, but he would only say he did what needed to be done.

British statesman and political thinker Edmund Burke once said, "The only thing necessary for the triumph of evil is for good men to do nothing." Like George F. R. Ellis, when we take such ideas to heart we are putting ourselves in position to become world-changers.[29]

Making a Life

*Be constantly renewed in the spirit of your mind — having a
fresh mental and spiritual attitude.*
Ephesians 4:23 AMP

No doubt we would all agree with the
sentiment: "There's more to life than things." Yet much
of our lives seem to be spent in the acquisition,
maintenance, and disposal of material goods. Certainly
we cannot enjoy the basics of food, shelter, and
clothing without a concern for things.

The truly important things of life, however, are
those which cannot be encountered by the physical
senses, purchased with money, or placed on a shelf.
When we take a look at what we value most in life we
generally find family, friends, health, peace,
contentment, laughter, helping others, and communion
with the Lord foremost on our list of priorities.

One of the ways to get at the "free" things in life is
to follow this advice of Sidney Lovett:

"Give the best you have received from the past to the best that you may come to know in the future.

"Accept life daily not as a cup to be drained but as a chalice to be filled with whatsoever things are honest, pure, lovely, and of good report. Making a living is best undertaken as part of the more important business of making a life.

"Every now and again take a good look at something not made with hands — a mountain, a star, the turn of a stream. There will come to you wisdom and patience and solace, and above all, the assurance that you are not alone in the world."[30]

Meditate on the "intangibles" as you spend this time alone with the Lord. Take a moment to stare out a window or sit in a garden, and undertake the important business of making a life!

Not Worth a Dime

There is nothing concealed that will not be disclosed, or hidden that will not be made known.

Luke 12:2

The story is told of a young man who was invited to preach at a church in Nashville, Tennessee. On an impulse he used as his text, "Thou shalt not steal."

The next morning he stepped onto a city bus and handed the driver a dollar bill. The driver handed him his change and he walked to the rear of the bus to stand, since there were no seats available.

Once he had steadied himself, he counted his change. There was a dime too much. His first thought was, *The bus company will never miss this dime.*

By now the bus had stopped again and the narrow aisle between him and the driver was one long line of people. Then it hit him, he could not keep money that did not belong to him.

A half dozen "excuse me's" and several scowling looks later, he had made his way to the front and said to the driver, "You gave me too much change."

The driver replied, "Yes, a dime too much. I gave it to you on purpose. You see, I heard your sermon yesterday, and I watched in my mirror as you counted your change. Had you kept the dime I would never again have had any confidence in preaching."

Imagine the outcome if this young man had decided the displeasure of his fellow passengers wasn't worth a dime's worth of honesty?

Our influence is like a shadow; it may fall even where we think we've never been. We also need to realize there are no "time-outs" or "vacations" we can take in keeping the Lord's commandments or being true to our conscience.

Stay on track with what you know is right!

Signposts

When my spirit was overwhelmed within me,
then thou knewest my path.
Psalm 142:3 KJV

One very dark night a man drove along a deserted road on his way to a place he had visited only once before. As he drove, he suddenly became uneasy, thinking he might have missed a turn two or three miles back.

He drove on mile after mile. Several times he slowed down, overcome by indecision. Should he turn around and drive back to that intersection, now ten miles behind him? If he was wrong, turning back would cost him an additional twenty or thirty minutes, and he was barely on schedule as it was.

Slower and slower he went. The tension built in his body as his hands gripped the steering wheel and a knot of stress between his shoulders began to throb.

He began to think, "Even if it's a mistake, I have to go back to reassure myself."

Just as he was about to turn around, his headlights reflected off a white marker in the distance. He increased his speed and soon saw the familiar shield that marks U.S. highways. The number 82 was clearly visible, and that was the road he needed to take. He continued on his way with confidence.

Sometimes in the dark nights of our travel through life, we feel we've missed a turn or read a sign incorrectly. Knowing our indecision, God often gives us reassuring signs to help us reestablish our heading and our confidence.

If you find yourself confused and directionless today, God has placed bright signposts in your path — the cross and empty tomb of Jesus Christ. In them you can see the greatest markers of His love, and you can continue on the path He sets before you with full confidence.

Such as I Have, I Give

Stir up the gift of God which is in you.
2 Timothy 1:6 NKJV

The word talent usually evokes images of great musicians, actors, and artists. When we think of talent in this limited sense, however, we feel untalented if we aren't gifted in any of these areas. The truth is, talents come in as many shapes and sizes as there are people, and God has given each of us one or more.

What are some of the "not-so-obvious" talents? Compassion is one. Do you feel kindness toward someone in a distressing situation? Then you have been given a talent! Use that feeling to write a letter of encouragement to someone you know who is in need. Do you like to plan surprises for people who may otherwise feel forgotten or left out? Then you are gifted! Don't bury that talent — use it to bring joy to another person.

Perhaps you have the gift of seeing something good in every individual. That is a gift all Christians need to cultivate. Affirm the good in someone, and then spread the "good news" about them. It usually takes someone else to see and bring out the best in people. You may see a talent in a person he or she doesn't even know about!

Do you have a calm spirit in the midst of calamity? Can you think clearly when surrounded by turmoil? Then you are gifted — and your talent is very much in need.

That was a talent Jesus demonstrated when He slept through the storm on a boat, didn't lose sight of His purpose when facing the angry crowd, and faced His death sentence on the cross.

Do you have a cup of cold water to offer another person? Then you have a gift. Use it in the name of Jesus and for the glory of God.

Now think again. What talents do you have?

Rise Gently And Slowly

So teach us to number our days,
that we may present to Thee
a heart of wisdom.
Psalm 90:12 NASB

Scuba diving is a sport that grows more and more popular every year. But those who take it up must be aware of the dangers it poses.

One of the biggest threats is decompression illness, or "the bends." While divers are underwater, they breathe compressed air; its pressure is equal to that of the water around them. If the diver stays down a long time and dives deeply, his body absorbs a great deal of compressed gas. If he then ascends too quickly, his body can't expel the extra gases slowly enough to avoid the formation of bubbles in his body tissues.

When bubbles form in the brain, spinal cord, or nerves outside the central nervous system, the results can be paralysis, convulsions, lack of coordination, numbness, nausea, speech defects, and personality changes.

Divers suffering from decompression must be recompressed in a hyperbaric chamber, and then gradually decompressed while breathing pure oxygen.

How can decompression be avoided? By ascending more slowly, with several interruptions along the way. Another method is taking a "safety stop" for several minutes at a depth of five or six meters.[31]

When it comes to our career, how quickly do we want to rise to the top? Is it worth getting "the bends" to arrive there faster than anyone else?

Each time you dive into your work at the beginning of the day, remember to gradually let go of it at the end of the day. Learn to wean yourself from it so you can relax and recuperate in the company of family or friends. Then you will get a good night's sleep before strapping on the tank bright and early the next morning.

Moments of Contentment

*I have learned how to be content (satisfied
to the point where I am not disturbed or
disquieted) in whatever state I am.*
Philippians 4:11 AMP

Lf anyone knew about "tornado days" — those
days when projects and deadlines fly around you in a
flurry — it was the apostle Paul. He wrote to the
Corinthians that in the course of his life he was beaten
to the point of death with whips and rods; stoned and
left for dead; shipwrecked; in peril from rivers, bandits,
and seas; sleepless and hungry; cold and without
adequate clothing; and persecuted virtually
everywhere he went. Yet he was able to say to the
Philippians, in essence, "I have learned to be in peace,
no matter what happens." Paul had learned the key to
inner contentment.

That peace, born of the Spirit in our hearts, is
something we should each cherish. When stressful

situations attempt to rob us of our peace, we need to ask the Lord to renew His presence within us. This prayer by Louis Bromfield seems to have been written for just those times:

> "*Oh, Lord, I thank you for the privilege and gift of living in a world filled with beauty and excitement and variety.*
>
> *I thank you for the gift of loving and being loved, for the friendliness and understanding and beauty of the animals on the farm and in the forest and marshes, for the green of the trees, the sound of a waterfall, the darting beauty of the trout in the brook.*
>
> *I thank you for the delights of music and children, of other men's thoughts and conversation and their books to read by the fireside or in bed with the rain falling on the roof or the snow blowing past outside the window.*"[32]

You may not be in a place where you have great beauty around you, but you can close your eyes and imagine yourself in such a place. Make that secret chamber of your heart your place of prayer, your place to experience contentment.

Small Things

He that is faithful in that which is least
is faithful also in much: and he that is unjust
in the least is unjust also in much.
Luke 16:10 KJV

In a certain bank there was a trust department in which four young men and one older man were employed. The directors decided to promote the older employee and then give one of the younger men his place as head of the department.

After considering the merits of each young man, the directors selected one of them for the new position and gave him a substantial increase in salary. They decided to notify him of the promotion that afternoon at four o'clock.

During the noon hour the young man went to a cafeteria for lunch. One of the directors was behind him in line, with several other customers between them. The director saw the young man select his food, including a piece of butter. He proceeded to hide the butter under other food and lied to the cashier about what was on his plate.

That afternoon the directors notified the young man that they had intended to give him a promotion, but because of what had been seen in the cafeteria, they would have to discharge him instead. They could not have someone who would lie and steal as head of their trust department.

What businesses call "employee theft" is often thought of by the employee as "borrowing." So open and prevalent are such "loans" that even committed Christians can fail to realize that what they are doing is stealing. And a few sheets of paper, pencils, long distance phone calls, Xerox copies, or extra time at lunch add up.

The next time you are tempted to "borrow" something from your employer, picture Jesus asking you where you got it!

His Way

May the Lord direct your hearts
into the love of God and into
the steadfastness of Christ.
2 Thessalonians 3:5 NASB

$\mathscr{D}$anish philosopher Sören Kierkegaard tells a parable about a wild duck. This duck was flying north one spring across the European continent. On the flight he stopped in a barnyard in Denmark, where some domestic ducks were being raised for food. Enjoying the food and security of the barnyard, he decided to stay for an hour, then a day, then a week, then a month, and finally all summer.

Summer eventually turned to autumn and his wild duck friends, heading south for the winter, flew overhead. This wild duck was stirred by his friends' cries, so he flapped his wings to fly up and join them in flight to warmer country for winter.

However, he quickly found that the delicious fare he had enjoyed all summer had made him so soft and heavy, he could not fly any higher than the roof of the barn. As he sank back to the ground he said to himself, "Oh well, my life is safe here and the food is good. I'll stay right where I am!"

Every spring, and then again every autumn, he heard the honking of the wild ducks as they flew over the barnyard. For a few seasons, he tried to join his mates, but the day came when he paid no attention to the wild ducks honking and flying overhead.

The story of the wild duck reminds us of poet William Wordsworth's words, "The world is too much with us; late and soon, getting and spending, we lay waste our powers."

The world's cares and comforts can easily distract us from God's purpose for our lives. There are many times when we have to force ourselves to do the right thing, keep in shape, and live balanced lives.

If we get sidetracked just as the wild duck did, we need to draw near to God. Like a magnet that has been demagnetized and has lost its ability to determine direction, we can get back on track by staying in close contact with the most powerful magnet in the universe, Jesus Christ. He never loses His sense of direction!

Escape Valve

*Be merciful — sympathetic, tender, responsive, and
compassionate — even as your Father is [all these].*
Luke 6:36 AMP

Have you just about had enough of that
domineering coworker? Is the boss on your case today?
Are you tired of the attitude of that person you can't
seem to avoid?

We all encounter people — sometimes on a frequent
basis — that we just don't like. And to make matters
worse, even those we do like can have a bad day!

Eleanor Roosevelt gave advice for that situation:

"A mature person is one who does not think only in
*absolutes, who is able to be objective even when deeply
stirred emotionally, who has learned that there is both good
and bad in all people and in all things, and who walks
humbly and deals charitably with the circumstances of life,
knowing that in this world no one is all knowing and
therefore all of us need both love and charity."*

Certainly we would all like to attain to such a level of maturity! But how? Jesus taught His followers in Luke 6:37 (AMP) there were three specific things they needed to do to get along with other people:

- *Judge not — neither pronouncing judgment nor subjecting to censure — and you will not be judged.* Don't speak ill of anyone, it only adds fuel to hard feelings. Instead, speak a word of encouragement to them.

- *Do not condemn and pronounce guilty, and you will not be condemned and pronounced guilty.* Don't "write off" someone as hopeless or without merit; don't snub them. That only creates more tension.

- *Acquit and forgive and release (give up resentment, let it drop), and you will be acquitted and forgiven and released.* Say to the Lord, "This person is Your child, and therefore Yours to discipline. Help them, and help me."

Refuse to let another person put you in a pressure cooker today. Release the "steam" you feel in acts of kindness and prayer.

They Already Knew Him

*Let your light so shine before men, that they may see your good
works, and glorify your Father which is in heaven.*
Matthew 5:16 KJV

A missionary was sent to a faraway land where
few Westerners had ever ventured. To anyone's
knowledge, no missionary had ever ministered in that
area, nor had the Gospel been preached. Therefore, he
decided to begin by explaining the story of Jesus Christ
in the most simple way possible.

Having painstakingly learned the language, he
gathered the village together to hear their first sermon
about a loving God. He told of the selfless love, infinite
compassion, merciful tenderness, and dynamic healing
power of Jesus. He was pleased to see how interested
the crowd was.

Then he noticed they were beginning to nod and
smile knowingly, as if they already knew the Man who

went about doing good. Delighted with their obvious interest and reception, he was nevertheless baffled by their recognition of Jesus as a person.

Finally he could contain his curiosity no longer. He asked how many in the audience had ever heard of this Man.

The response was overwhelming. It seemed they all knew Him! Astonished, he asked, "How? When? Who told you about Him?"

"He used to live among us!" an older gentleman said. "We called him Doctor, but he was as you've described him exactly."

As it turned out, the village had once had the services of a patient and loving Christian physician. He lived among them and took care of them in sickness and health for many years. So strong was his simple, Christlike love and care, the villagers had mistaken him for the Savior the missionary described.

Determine to live your life in such a way that even the lost would recognize Jesus in you!

The Empty Tomb

*Be honest in your judgment and do not
decide at a glance — superficially and by
appearances; but judge fairly and righteously.*
John 7:24 AMP

Philip was born a mongoloid. He was a happy
child, but as he grew older he became increasingly
aware that he was different from other children.

Philip went to Sunday school with boys and girls
his own age. The class had wonderful experiences
together — learning, laughing, playing. But Philip
remained an outsider.

As an Easter lesson, the Sunday school teacher
gave each student a large egg-shaped plastic container.
Each child was to explore the church grounds and find
something that symbolized new life to them, put it in
their "egg," and bring it back to share with the class.

The children had a grand time running about the church yard collecting symbols. Then they gathered back in the classroom, put their eggs on the table, and watched with great anticipation as the teacher opened each egg. In one egg, there was a flower, in another a butterfly. The students responded with great glee and enthusiasm as the teacher revealed the contents of each egg...a branch, a leaf, a flower bud.

When the teacher opened the next egg, there was nothing in it. As could be expected, the eight-year-olds responded, "That's not fair — that's stupid! Somebody didn't do it right."

Philip went up to the teacher, tugged on her sleeve, and said, "It's mine. That egg is mine." The children laughed and said, "You never do anything right, Philip. There's nothing there."

Philip replied, "I did so do it. I did do it. It's empty — the tomb is empty!"

The classroom fell silent. From that day on things were different. Philip became a full-fledged part of the class. The children took him into their friendship. Philip had been freed from the tomb of his being different and given a new life among his peers.[33]

How Does Your Heart Rate?

Man looks at the outward appearance,
but the Lord looks at the heart.
1 Samuel 16:7

A recent medical study measured the effects of mental stress on blood pressure. The results were surprising: If your blood pressure goes sky high during a "mental challenge," you are a prime candidate for hardening of the arteries, which can cause strokes and heart attacks.

Researchers used a tricky computer game to test their theory. Words for colors were written in color, and the 348 volunteers had to identify the color in which the words were written. To make things more difficult, the computer sped up the game to guarantee everyone would have a seventeen percent error rate. Blood pressure monitors recorded the effects.

Over the next two years, researchers used ultrasound to check for obstruction in the volunteers' carotid arteries (blood vessels that feed the brain). Those volunteers whose blood pressure soared during the computer game had a higher rate of obstruction in their arteries.

Hardening of the arteries can cause physical death, but hardening our heart toward God and toward others can destroy something much more important than our bodies — our ability to live fulfilling lives and be effective witnesses for Jesus Christ in this world.

As much as we need to take care of our health and learn to cope with stress, we should be even more concerned with what God sees when He looks into our hearts. Are we soft and malleable, or hard and unyielding?

"Love one another deeply, from the heart," says 1 Peter 1:22 (NIV). That's the best exercise our hearts can have!

The Ripple Effect

Which [the mustard seed] indeed is the least
of all seeds: but when it is grown, it is the
greatest among herbs, and becometh a tree,
so that the birds of the air come
and lodge in the branches thereof.
Matthew 13:32 KJV

Not everyone who commits his life to Jesus Christ will be called to be world famous. The majority of us are called to fulfill less noticeable roles in our churches, communities, and families. Yet only God may know how significant our roles are to the future of thousands — even millions.

A century and a half ago a humble minister lived and died in a small village in Leicestershire, England. He lived there his entire life and never traveled far from home. He never attended college, had no formal degrees, but was a faithful village minister.

The Ripple Effect

In his congregation was a young cobbler to whom he gave special attention, teaching him the Word of God. This young man was William Carey, later hailed as one of the greatest missionaries of modern times.

The village minister also had a son — a boy whom he taught faithfully and constantly encouraged. The boy's character and talents were profoundly impacted by his father's life. That son grew up to be a man many considered the mightiest public orator of his day: Robert Hall. Widely admired for his saintly character, his preaching was powerful and his sermons influenced the decisions of statesmen.

It seems the village pastor accomplished little in his life as a preacher. There were no spectacular revivals, great miracles, or major church growth. But his faithful witness and godly life had much to do with giving India its Carey and England its Robert Hall.

When you think you are having no impact in the world by teaching a Sunday school class or visiting those who are homebound, remember the little country preacher who influenced two nations for the Lord.

In Progress

He who has begun a good work in you
will complete it until the day of Jesus Christ.
Philippians 1:6 NKJV

A sign in a hotel lobby that was being remodeled stated, "Please be patient. Renovation in progress to produce something new and wonderful." Perhaps we all need to wear a sign like that! We are all unfinished projects under construction, being made into something wonderful. Being mindful of this, we might have greater grace and patience for others, as well as for ourselves, while the work is underway.

Hope is the anticipation of good. Like the hotel lobby in the disarray of renovation, our hope is often in spite of our present circumstances. What is the basis for our hope?

For the Christian, hope is not simple optimism or a denial of reality. The reason for our hope is Jesus

Christ, the solid rock of our faith. As the hymn writer wrote, "My hope is built on nothing less than Jesus' blood and righteousness." We are never without hope for our lives if we know the Lord Jesus.

The focus of our hope is to be like Jesus. That goal may seem too great and way beyond our ability to achieve, and it is. How do we reach that goal?

The Scriptures tell us it is "Christ in you" that is our hope. (See Colossians 1:27.) The transformation of our lives into Christlikeness is a goal that is larger than life. As Paul wrote to the Corinthians, to have hope only for this life is to be miserable. (See 1 Corinthians 15:19.) The Christian hope is for this life *and* for eternity.

A little chapel in the hills of the Scottish Highlands has a sign chiseled in Gaelic on the front door. Translated into English it says: "Come as you are, but don't leave as you came." When we come to Jesus we can come as we are. But He will not leave us the same. That is our sure hope.[34]

Come On Up

Day and night they kept close watch on the city gates in order to kill him. But his followers took him by night and lowered him in a basket through an opening in the wall.

Acts 9:23-25

Ice climbing is perhaps the most dangerous specialty in mountain climbing — but it's one that some climbers *choose* to do! The most challenging are frozen waterfalls. One climber described them this way: 60 to 70 feet wide and about 200 feet from base to clifftop.

Every ice climber wears crampons, a steel frame with spikes that straps to their boots. The first order of business for prospective climbers is to learn to move from side to side on an ice wall while wearing crampons.

Next comes technique. Each style applies to a different phase of the climb and involves the placement of the boots parallel to the ice (French); one boot toe pointed in and one boot parallel (American); and finally, both boot tips jammed into the ice (German).

Some walls have a lower-grade pitch — twenty to thirty degrees. It is tougher to climb when the pitch is thirty-five to sixty degrees, and even more difficult between sixty and ninety degrees. At ninety degrees, a climber has to haul himself up with his whole body — arm strength alone is not enough.

Ice climbers also wear a safety harness, with one end of a rope threaded through it. The other end of the rope is fastened securely at the top of the wall, where other team members anticipate a fall and take some of the slack out of the rope, preventing serious injuries to the climber.[35]

Isn't that how it is in many endeavors? We think we only need to use one technique or that our strength alone will help us get by. Then we realize we must pray, study God's Word, and learn to lean on other believers from time to time to make it to the top. We can gather all the right equipment to climb the wall — crampons, ax, hammer, warm clothing, and gloves — but it's not enough.

As we scale our chosen wall each day, it's comforting to know Someone at the top is holding onto our rope too!

Expertise

*Study and be eager and do your utmost to present yourself to
God approved (tested by trial), a workman who has no cause to
be ashamed, correctly analyzing and accurately dividing —
rightly handling and skillfully teaching — the Word of Truth.*
2 *Timothy* 2:15 AMP

The story is told of a postgraduate student who
went to the great naturalist Agassiz to receive the
finishing touches on his education. The student had
many honors to his credit and was expecting a noble
assignment. He was more than a little surprised when
Agassiz gave him a small fish and told him to describe
it. The student replied, "That's only a sunfish."

Agassiz said, "I know that. Write a description of it."

Within a few minutes the student returned with
the description of the fish according to formal Latin
terminology, and provided the genus and family in
which the fish might be found on a chart. Agassiz read

what the student had written and then said, "Describe the fish for me."

The student then produced a four-page essay. Agassiz again told him to look at the fish and describe it. This continued for three weeks, by which time the fish was in an advanced state of decomposition. But the student had to admit, by then he really *knew* something about the fish. And Agassiz agreed.[36]

One modern-day philosopher has concluded that if you were to study only one small item, plant, or creature for five minutes a day for the next twenty years, you would be the world's foremost expert on that subject!

How important it is, then, that we spend time every day learning the most important lessons of all — those found in God's Word. If you really want to *know* what God says about how to live a successful life on this earth, make Bible reading a part of every day.

Do-It-Yourself Misery

Deceit is in the heart of them that imagine evil:
but to the counsellors of peace is joy.
Proverbs 12:20 KJV

Some people just can't figure out why life has dealt them such a miserable hand. They see others around them enjoying life, and that only adds to their misery. They're convinced their horrible lot in this world is a plot by others to keep them down. In truth, misery is always self-concocted. Here's a sure-fire recipe for misery printed in *The Gospel Herald*:

Think about yourself.
Talk about yourself.
Use "I" as often as possible.
Mirror yourself continually in the opinion of others.
Listen greedily to what people say about you.
Be suspicious.
Expect to be appreciated.

Be jealous and envious.

Be sensitive to slights.

Never forgive a criticism.

Trust nobody but yourself.

Insist on consideration and the proper respect.

Demand agreement with your own views on everything.

Sulk if people are not grateful to you for favors shown them.

Never forget a service you may have rendered.

Be on the lookout for a good time for yourself.

Shirk your duties if you can.

Do as little as possible for others.

Love yourself supremely.

Be selfish.[37]

This recipe is guaranteed to work. In fact, you don't even need all the ingredients to achieve total misery.

On the other hand, if misery's not your idea of a good time, do just the opposite. You'll have a hard time feeling even a little blue!

When Life Becomes Routine

Come unto me, all ye that labour and are heavy laden.
Matthew 11:28 KJV

Some days seem absent of purpose and motivation. On such a day, you might feel as this man felt:

"When I woke up this morning, I said to myself that this would be a day just like every other day. And it was. I took the same train as every morning, I read the same comments in the paper on an international situation which never changes. On my desk I found the same piles of papers to go through.

"The people all look the same and so does my supervisor. They had that blank expression which says that nothing new is going to happen today. For lunch I had the same old thing to eat. I went back to my desk until five o'clock. And then I just came home, knowing full well that tomorrow it will start all over again.

"God, I'm tired of it all. I had hoped for something completely different. I had dreamed that some day I would lead an active and exciting life. I'll never be anything but what I am. That was a dream."

When you begin to experience this kind of fatigue and boredom, it is time to take a break! These are symptoms of oncoming depression, and depression will keep you from living the full life God has planned for you.

To defeat fatigue, boredom, and depression, turn immediately to the Lord for a change of attitude, strength, and wisdom. Admit your dissatisfaction and frustration, be honest — He knows everything about you anyway!

Then listen for the answer. Chances are, you have fallen into destructive thought patterns and it's time to "cast down vain imaginations" (see 2 Corinthians 10:5). God may also be nudging you to try something new, as a profession, in ministry, as a hobby, or as a family activity.

One thing is certain, God does not want you to abandon the dreams He has given you. He wants you to fulfill the dreams He has put in your heart!

A "Body of Work"

Christ Jesus...gave Himself on our behalf that He might redeem
us (purchase our freedom) from all iniquity and purify for
Himself a people — to be peculiarly His own.
Titus 2:13-14 AMP

Sixty-five years has within it exactly 569,400 hours. If you subtract the number of hours that a person spends growing up and receiving a basic high-school education, and then subtract the hours that people normally spend eating, sleeping, and engaging in recreation, you will still have 134,000 hours for work between the ages of 18 and 65.

That's a lot of time! Yet, many people reach retirement age, look back over their years, and conclude: "I was only putting in time and drawing a paycheck."

Take a different approach, starting today. Choose to create a "body of work" with the time that you have!

A "Body of Work"

A body of work is more than a career or a pile of achievements, awards, and accomplishments. A "body" of work is just that — physical and human. A body of work is *people*.

King David desired to build a great temple for the Lord. The prophet Nathan came to Him with God's Word on the idea: "The Lord declares to you that He will make for you a house." David had in mind mortar and cedar. The Lord had in mind family and relationships! (See 2 Samuel 7.)

Get to know the people with whom you work. Spend time with them. Value them. Share experiences with them. Be there when they face crises and when they celebrate milestones. Count your colleagues — and also those above and below you on the organizational ladder — among your friends, and treat them *as* friends. Build relationships that endure through the years, regardless of who is transferred, promoted, or laid off. *People* are what will matter to you far more than possessions when you reach your retirement years.

"Fussing" Away Time

Therefore do not worry about tomorrow,
for tomorrow will worry about itself.
Each day has enough trouble of its own.
Matthew 6:34

There was a dear old lady from the country who was going on a railway journey the first time. She was to travel about fifty miles through an interesting and beautiful region and had looked forward to this trip with great pleasure. However, once she boarded the train it took her so long to get her baskets and parcels right, her seat comfortably arranged, the shades and shutters right, the anxious questions about all the things she had left behind answered, that she was just settling down to enjoy the trip when they called out the name of her station!

"Oh my!" she said, "if I had only known that we would be there so soon, I wouldn't have wasted my time in fussing. I hardly saw the scenery!"

"Fussing" Away Time

Continuing to "fuss" with things left behind yesterday and things yet to do tomorrow robs us of the joys God brings to us today. If you've said, "I'm too busy to..." several times today, it might be time to review your priorities.

Too Busy

Too busy to read the Bible
Too busy to wait and pray!
Too busy to speak out kindly
To someone by the way!

Too busy to care and struggle,
To think of the life to come!
Too busy building mansions,
To plan for the Heavenly Home.

Too busy to help a brother
Who faces the winter blast!
Too busy to share his burden
When self in the balance is cast.

Too busy for all that is holy
On earth beneath the sky
Too busy to serve the Master
But not too busy to die.

Author Unknown

Give Me a Word

And the Word was God.
John 1:1 NKJV

Marjorie Holmes writes in *Lord, Let Me Love,* about her daughter, who had a fascination with words at a young age. From her earliest attempts at talking, she liked to try out new words and sounds. Often she would chant and sing words, or make up strange combinations of sounds to build her own vocabulary.

She was impatient, however, because all the things she was learning far exceeded her ability to express them. Because she needed more words, she began asking her mother for words, just like she might ask her for a cookie or a hug.

The little girl would ask, "Give me a bright word, Mother." Marjorie would answer with a string of nouns and adjectives that described the word *bright*, such as "sunshine, golden, luminous, shiny, sparkling."

Then she would ask for a soft word. Marjorie responded, "Velvety soft like a blackberry or a pony's nose. Or furry, like your kitten. Or how about a lullaby?" And when she was angry, she would demand a glad word. The game continued until the little girl's attitude was transformed by the happy thoughts prompted by happy words.[38]

Through words, God spoke creation into being. He said, "Let there be light." And there was light. He said, "Let us make the earth and the fullness of it." And foliage, animals, birds, and fish were created.

God gave us His Word so we could live full and satisfying lives while we are here on earth. The Bible is teeming with wonderful, powerful, beautiful words for our daily lives.

What word do you need today? Do you need a glad word or a comforting word? "Give me a word," can be the prayer of your heart to God during your coffee break — then open your Bible and let Him speak!

Stay Sharp

See, I am doing a new thing! Now it springs up;
do you not perceive it? I am making a way
in the desert and streams in the wasteland.
Isaiah 43:19

$\mathscr{I}$f you think you have trouble keeping up with changes in *your* line of work, consider the laparoscopic surgeon. Since the primary goal of modern Western medicine is to correct a problem in a noninvasive manner and with as short a hospital stay as possible, these doctors are being forced to learn new techniques practically overnight.

The solution? Something called "boot camp" for physicians. It's the brainchild of James C. Rooser, Jr., director of endolaparoscopic surgery at Yale University School of Medicine.

In laparoscopy, surgical instruments and a camera can enter the body through a smaller-than-usual incision. Surgeons can see the instruments on a TV monitor, and must operate by keeping a close eye on the screen and a firm grasp on their tools. In boot camp, surgeons improve these crucial skills by playing a series of arduous games.

In "Slam Dunk," the nondominant hand must use a pair of miniature tweezers attached to a shaft — its bottom end hidden in a box — to pick up black-eyed peas. Watching the screen, the surgeon uses a handle on the top end of the shaft to control the tweezers and drop each pea into a tiny hole.

Other equally difficult games also place emphasis on the use of the nondominant hand, and focus on building confidence, as opposed to out-of-control arrogance, in the operating room.[39]

When it comes to mastering a new skill in your work, it's important that you continue to be open to new ideas and new ways of doing things. Sometimes it pays to stop what you are doing and master a new skill.

During your prayer time today, ask the Lord to show you a new thing!

Enjoy the Process

Work in quiet fashion...do not grow weary of doing good.
2 Thessalonians 3:12-13 NASB

We all would love to love our work! That's the conclusion of numerous marketplace researchers, who seem universally to prescribe: If you don't like the work you are doing, decide what you like doing and then work at that. For many people, that advice falls under the "easier said than done" category.

How can we add pleasure to a job that may have become boring, frustrating, or discouraging? Begin by reflecting on those for whom you are working. First and foremost, you are working for the Lord. Secondly, for yourself — for maintenance of body and possessions, as well as self-esteem. Thirdly, you are working for other people — your family members, but also those who benefit from your charitable contributions. Lastly, you are working for a company or cause — which in "real-people" terms comes down to those with whom you work on a daily basis.

With people as your mind set, try engaging in these pleasure-boosters related to your job:

1. Make a small monthly contribution to a charity that serves people whom you encounter regularly — perhaps the homeless you see on your way to work.

2. Give at least ten genuine compliments a day to those with whom you work. Voice appreciation for their appearance, work, and kindness.

3. Keep a photograph of your loved ones with you and spend a few moments each day looking at it. Say a little prayer for them.

4. Set your own personal goals about productivity, quality, and efficiency. Then reward yourself in a small way on each day you surpass your goals. Document your improvement — your record may lead to a new and better position!

These simple reminders about *why* you work and *who* benefits from your work, can help put more meaning into your job. And with more meaning comes a sense of personal satisfaction, which is nearly always translated into "enjoyment."

So Send I You

Also I heard the voice of the Lord, saying,
Whom shall I send, and who will go for us?
Then said I, Here am I; send me.
Isaiah 6:8 KJV

Margaret Clarkson was a 23-year-old school teacher in a gold-mining town in northern Ontario, Canada — far from friends and family. As she meditated on John 20:21 one evening, God spoke to her through the phrase "So send I you." She realized that this lonely area was the place to which "God had sent her." This was her mission field. As she quickly set down her thoughts in verse, one of the finest and most popular missionary hymns of the twentieth century was born.

Because of a physical disability, Miss Clarkson was unable to fulfill her early desire of going to a foreign mission field. Yet her words have challenged many to respond to God's call for service:

So Send I You

So send I you to labor unrewarded,
To serve unpaid, unloved, unsought, unknown,
To bear rebuke, to suffer scorn and scoffing —
So send I you to suffer for My sake.

So send I you to bind the bruised and broken,
O'er wand'ring souls to work, to weep, to wake,
To bear the burdens of a world a-weary —
So send I you to suffer for My sake.

So send I you to loneliness and longing,
With heart ahung'ring for the loved and known,
Forsaking home and kindred, friend and dear one —
So send I you to know my love alone.

So send I you to leave your life's ambition,
To die to dear desire, self-will resign,
To labor long and love where men revile you —
So send I you to lose your life in Mine.

So send I you to hearts made hard by hatred,
To eyes made blind because they will not see,
To spend — tho' it be blood — to spend and spare not —
So send I you to taste of Calvary.[40]

"As the Father hath sent Me, so send I you" (John 20:21).

Sowing Peace

Blessed are the peacemakers,
for they shall be called sons of God.
Matthew 5:9 RSV

The entire European continent felt the blows of hatred delivered by the evil tyrant Adolf Hitler. Millions of people died as a result of his platform of hate; millions more were scarred for life.

Heinz was an eleven-year-old Jewish boy who lived with his family in the Barvarian village of Furth during the 1930s. When Hitler's band of thugs came tearing through the village, Heinz's father lost his job as a schoolteacher, recreational activities were forbidden, and Furth's streets became battlegrounds.

Neighborhoods were terrorized by the Hitler youth looking to make trouble. The young Heinz always kept alert to stay clear of them. When he saw them coming, he sought cover to get out of their way.

Sowing Peace

One day, Heinz couldn't avoid a face-to-face encounter with a Hitler bully. A brutal beating seemed inevitable, but Heinz walked away from the fray without a scratch. This time he used his persuasive abilities and language skills to convince his enemy that a fight was not necessary. This would not be the last time this young Jewish boy would use his peacemaking skill in Hitler-occupied Europe.

Eventually Heinz and his family escaped to safety in America, where Heinz would make his mark. He became known as a mediator and peacemaker among world leaders and nations. The young boy who grew up as Heinz anglicized his name when he came to America. We know him as Henry Kissinger.

Today put your talents to use as a peacemaker to work together with those of different opinions. When you sow seeds of peace you are doing God's work on earth and you will reap a harvest of goodness.

Keep It Moving

For in him we live and move and have our being.
Acts 17:28

The Masai, a nomadic people of East Africa, vividly illustrate the importance of reevaluating your position from time to time and knowing when to move on.

On the move all year long, the Masai live mostly on the meat and milk of their herds. They stay in one place as long as the rain lasts. Natural ecologists, they leave an area before its resources are totally depleted and return after the land has had time to recover.

Sadly, this aspect of the Masai lifestyle may soon be a thing of the past. Governments are encouraging the Masai to settle in one area. But when the land is exhausted and the herds start to die, the Masai often find themselves forced to sell their land and find a new home. The Masai are herdsmen, not farmers. The grasslands they need are not easily bordered by fences and they have no tradition of planting or irrigation.[41]

Most of us do not farm or have herds that need grazing land. But we do live lives that sometimes deplete all the "resources" a particular job or position can give us. Often we grow beyond the challenge a job provides, or we develop our skills to a level that they are no longer challenged — or rewarded — in the only position available to us. Then too, doing the same thing for a long period of time is not only exhausting to the body, but also to the mind and spirit. A time comes when we need to "move on."

Certainly the children of Israel knew this as they wandered in the wilderness. They were led by a pillar of cloud by day and of fire by night. When the pillar began to move, so did they! (See Nehemiah 9:12.)

We can each use a periodic evaluation. Every now and then, we need to look at what we are doing and ask ourselves if it isn't time to find a constructive way to move on to new challenges, a new position, or a new career.

Stress Levels

The work of righteousness shall be peace.
Isaiah 32:17 KJV

Health activists in Japan say that overwork kills 30,000 workers every year in that country. They even have a word for it — "karoshi." In America, 50 percent of all deaths each year are attributed to hypertension and stress-related illnesses. Thirty percent of the population suffers from stress-related health problems ranging from poor immune function to high blood pressure and heart disease.

Under stress, our hearts race, muscles contract, arteries narrow, and our blood thickens. All these physical responses provide the rush you need that could help save your life in a life-threatening encounter. But our bodies were not made to operate at these unrelenting levels 24 hours a day.

A recent study of successful professionals revealed that they practiced stress-management techniques.

Praying, walking on the beach, stroking the household pet, working out at the gym, or taking a long bubble bath all helped them to gain a sense of inner well-being and peace. The important point was not that they were devoted to any one regimen — or that one technique worked for all people — but each person had discovered his or her own technique for relaxing.

Jesus promised His disciples, "Peace I leave with you; my peace I give you. I do not give to you as the world gives. Do not let your hearts be troubled and do not be afraid" (John 14:27). The inner peace Jesus gives us does not mean we will never experience conflict or difficulty. The peace that Jesus gives is the peace of reconciliation with God, unity with other Christians, and living at peace with the world around us. Within that peace, we still need creative ways of letting the stress melt away from our lives. We need to *learn* new ways to relax.[42]

Offerings

May He remember all your meal offerings,
and find your burnt offering acceptable!
Psalm 20:3 NASB

*T*he Israelites had an elaborate system of sacrifices and offerings, all of which were commanded by God for specific times and seasons. When they offered money, grain, or animals to the Lord, is was an act of worship. What offerings do we give in worship today?

Saint Francis of Assisi was hoeing his garden one day when someone asked him what he would do if he were to learn he was going to die before sunset. He replied, "I would finish hoeing my garden." Saint Francis saw his life as an offering to the Lord — an outpouring of his time, energy, and love that constituted many expressions, including his work.

When we regard everything we do as being "for the Lord," then everything we do becomes an offering. We seek to act toward others in a way that is pleasing to

Him. We do good deeds for others — including putting in a good day's work — because that is what He asks of us.

Using the same analogy of a garden, Julian of Norwich pointed toward a second form of sacrifice:

Be a gardener.
Dig a ditch, toil and sweat,
And turn the earth upside down
And seek the deepness
And water the plants in time.
Continue this labor
And make sweet floods to run
And noble and abundant fruits to spring.
Take this food and drink
And carry it to God as your true worship.[43]

Consider the activities of your day and how they can be an offering of love and thanksgiving to the Lord. When we do all things for Him, even the most difficult tasks become a joy!

Make Hay While the Sun Shines

This is what the Lord says: "Stand at the crossroads and look;
ask for the ancient paths, ask where the good way is,
and walk in it, and you will find rest for your souls."
Jeremiah 6:16

Medicine. What a glamorous profession. High salaries, prestige, respect, travel, speaking engagements, curing the sick, discovering new drugs.

Medicine. Occasional tedium, exposure to a host of diseases, making an incorrect diagnosis, watching patients die, long hours, no sleep, no family time, malpractice suits.

Medicine. Maybe not so glamorous after all.

When a doctor spends most of the year trying to help their patients sort out various physical and mental ailments, while trying not to become emotionally involved, where do they go to heal their own wounded spirit?

One doctor in Michigan goes back home to Vermont to help her father and brother with the haying. It's elegantly simple work, she says. The job has a set of basic steps which, when followed, result in neatly bound bales of hay that are then trucked off the fields and sold the following winter. Haying is hot, sweaty, tiring work, but it has a satisfying, beginning, middle, and end...unlike medicine.[44]

All of us need an activity that is the antithesis of what we do all day. We need a cobweb-clearer, a routine-shaker.

Those who engage in "mental" work all day often find crafts or hobbies that involve their hands to be very rewarding and enjoyable. Conversely, those who engage in hard manual labor often enjoy working puzzles, reading, or engaging in a course of study.

Those who work with people in high-stress environments frequently find great pleasure in gardening or other solitary activities. Those who work alone often enjoy spending their off hours with other people.

We each need to be completely out of our normal work mode for a little while every day — and for a week or two when we can manage it. It's a crucial part of living a balanced life!

The Crowded Ways

Defend the poor and fatherless: do justice
to the afflicted and needy. Deliver the poor and needy:
rid them out of the hand of the wicked.
Psalm 82:3-4 KJV

*H*enry David Thoreau, noted American writer, philosopher, and naturalist of the nineteenth century, once described the city as "a place where people are lonely together," a loneliness he attributed to a lack of caring relationships.

If Thoreau's observation was true in the past, it is truer in the present, and the prediction is that it will become alarmingly more so in the near future. In 1950 there were only seven cities in the world with more than five million people. Two of them were in Third World countries. Today there are 34 cities with more than five million people, 22 of which are in the Third World. By the year 2050 there will be nearly 100 cities with at least five million people, 80 of these in Africa, Asia, and Latin America. Twenty percent of the world's population will be living in the slums and squatter settlements of Third World countries.

The hymn "Where Cross the Crowded Ways of Life" was written in 1903 by a Methodist minister pastoring in New York City. The words draw our attention to the mission field that exists in the cities where we live. They read in part:

Where cross the crowded ways of life,
Where sound the cries of race and clan,
Above the noise of selfish strife,
We hear Thy voice, O Son of man!
The cup of water giv'n for Thee
Still holds the freshness of Thy grace;
Yet long these multitudes to see
The sweet compassion of Thy face.
O Master, from the mountain side,
Make haste to heal these hearts of pain;
Among these restless throngs abide;
O tread the city streets again:
Till sons of men shall learn Thy love
And follow where Thy feet have trod;
Till glorious, from Thy heav'n above,
Shall come the city of our God.[45]

Daily Bread

We do not have a High Priest who cannot
sympathize with our weakness, but was in all
points tempted as we are, yet without sin.
Hebrews 4:15 NKJV

The Lord Jesus knows our need for physical and spiritual nourishment. He knows we can't make it on our own, that in depending on our own resources we don't have what it takes for everyday life — let alone for everlasting life. In fact, we were created to depend on Him.

When Jesus instituted the Last Supper, He told His disciples to "do this in remembrance of Me." Remembering someone is to allow them to shape and influence our lives. Jesus was asking His disciples to remember Him in the Lord's Supper so that even when He was no longer physically present with them, He would still be shaping and guiding their lives. When we go to the Lord's Table, we give witness to the fact we are depending upon Jesus.

As we remember Jesus, we have the picture of Him giving himself to us to nurture and feed our souls. A song written by Arden Autry describes how He lovingly gave — and continues to give — His life for us:

As you eat this bread, as you drink this cup,
Let your heart give thanks and be lifted up.
Your soul can rest in this truth secure:
As you eat this bread, all I am is yours.

All I am is yours. All I am I gave,
Dying on the cross, rising from the grave,
Your sins to bear and your life restore:
As you eat this bread, all I am is yours.

In delight and joy, in the depths of pain,
In the anxious hours, through all loss and gain,
Your world may shake, but my Word endures:
As you eat this bread, all I am is yours.[46]

During this coffee break and throughout your day, remember Jesus. Let Him direct your thoughts and ways. It is His strength and wisdom that will give you success and fulfillment in life.

References

Unless otherwise indicated, all Scripture quotations are taken from the *Holy Bible, New International Version®* NIV®. Copyright © 1973, 1978, 1984 by International Bible Society. Used by permission of Zondervan Publishing House. All rights reserved.

Scripture quotations marked KJV are taken from the *King James Version* of the Bible.

Scripture quotations marked AMP are taken from *The Amplified Bible, Old Testament.* Copyright © 1965 by Zondervan Publishing House, Grand Rapids, Michigan. *New Testament* copyright © 1958 by The Lockman Foundation, La Habra, California. Used by permission.

Scripture quotations marked NKJV are taken from *The New King James Version* of the Bible. Copyright © 1979, 1980, 1982, 1994 by Thomas Nelson, Inc., Publishers. Used by permission.

Scripture quotations marked NASB are taken from the *New American Standard Bible.* Copyright © 1960, 1962, 1963, 1968, 1971, 1972, 1973, 1975, 1977 by The Lockman Foundation. Used by permission.

Endnotes

[1] *Illustrations for Preaching & Teaching*, Craig B. Larson, (Grand Rapids, MI: Baker Book House, 1993), p. 187.

[2] *A Guide to Prayer for All God's People*, Rueben P. Job and Norman Shawchuck, ed. (Nashville: Upper Room Books, 1990), pp. 255-256.

[3] *Illustrations Unlimited* James S. Hewett, ed. (Wheaton: Tyndale House, 1988), p. 19.

[4] *Worldwide Challenge*, January 1978, pp. 39-40.

[5] *Good Housekeeping,* February 1996, p. 20.

[6] *Encyclopedia Judaica*, Prof. Cecil Roth and Dr. Geoffrey Wigoder, eds. (Jerusalem: Kefer Publishing House, 1972), Vol. 4, pp. 142-143.

[7] *Illustrations for Preaching & Teaching*, Craig B. Larson (Grand Rapids, MI: Baker Book House, 1993), p. 106.

[8] *Spiritual Fitness*, Doris Donnelly (San Francisco: Harper, 1993), p. 111-124.

[9] "Leisure," *The Family Book of Best Loved Poems*, David L. George, ed. (Garden City, NY: Doubleday & Co., 1952), p. 261.

[10] *JAMA*, December 6, 1995, p. 21.

[11] *Illustrations for Preaching & Teaching,* Craig B. Larson (Grand Rapids, MI: Baker Book House, 1993), p. 122.

[12] *I Like This Poem*, Kaye Webb, ed. (Middlesex, England: Penguin Books, 1979), pp. 156-157.

[13] *The Treasure Chest,* Brian Culhane, ed. (San Francisco: Harper, 1995), p. 162.

[14]*Illustrations for Preaching & Teaching*, Craig B. Larson (Grand Rapids, MI: Baker Book House, 1993), p. 190.

[15]*Illustrations Unlimited*, James S. Hewett (Wheaton, IL: Tyndale House Publishers, 1988), p. 40.

[16]*Treasury of the Christian Faith*, Stanley Stuber and Thomas Clark, ed. (NY: Association Press, 1949), p. 355.

[17]*The Treasure Chest,* Brian Culhane, ed. (San Francisco: Harper, 1995), p. 162.

[18]*Illustrations Unlimited*, James S. Hewett (Wheaton, IL: Tyndale House Publishers, 1988), p. 496.

[19]*The Treasure Chest*, Brian Culhane, ed. (San Francisco: Harper, 1995), p. 171.

[20]*The Complete Book of Christian Prayer*, editor (NY: Continuum), 1995, p. 321.

[21]*Knight's Master Book of 4,000 Illustrations,* Walter B. Knight (Grand Rapids, MI: William B. Eerdmans Publishing Co., 1956), p. 64.

[22]*llustrations Unlimited* James S. Hewett, ed. (Wheaton: Tyndale House, 1988), pp. 15, 18, 279-280.

[23]*Knight's Master Book of 4,000 Illustrations,* Walter B. Knight, (Grand Rapids, MI: William B. Eerdmans Publishing Co., 1956), p. 71.

[24]*Newsweek*, March 6, 1995, pp. 60-61.

[25]*The Treasure Chest*, Brian Culhane, ed. (San Francisco: Harper, 1995), p. 171.

[26]Ibid., p. 177.

[27]*Macartney's Illustrations,* Clarence E. Macartney (NY:Abingdon Press, 1945, 1946), pp. 19, 172.

[28]*God's Song in My Heart*, Ruth Youngdahl Nelson (Philadelphia: Fortress Press, 1957), p. 248-249.

[29]*Scientific American,* October 1995, p. 50.

[30]*The Treasure Chest,* Brian Culhane, ed. (San Francisco, Harper, 1995), p. 176.

[31]*Scientific American*, August 1995, p. 70-77.

[32]*The Treasure Chest*, Brian Culhane, ed. (San Francisco: Harper, 1995), p. 188.

[33]*A Guide to Prayer for All God's People,* Rueben P. Job and Norman Shawchuck, ed. (Nashville: Upper Room Books, 1990), pp. 326-328.

[34]*Silent Strength For My Life*, Lloyd John Ogilvie (Eugene, OR: Harvest House Publishers, 1990), p. 113.

[35]*Westways*, March 1996, p. 19-21.

[36]*The Treasure Chest*, Brian Culhane, ed. (San Francisco: Harper, 1995), p. 200.

[37]*Knight's Master Book of 4,000 Illustrations,* Walter B. Knight (Grand Rapids, MI: William B. Eerdmans Publishing Co., 1956), p. 615.

[38]*Lord, Let Me Love*, Marjorie Holmes (NY: Doubleday, date), pp. 104-105.

[39]*Scientific American,* September 1995, p. 24.

[40]*Amazing Grace*, Kenneth W. Osbeck (Grand Rapids, MI: Kregel Publications, 1990), p. 38.

[41]*Scientific American*, January 1994, p. 159.

[42]*Newsweek*, March 6, 1995, p. 62.

[43]*The Treasure Chest,* Brian Culhane, ed. (San Francisco: Harper, 1995), p. 204.

[44]*JAMA*, January 10. 1996, p. 99.

[45]*Amazing Grace*, Kenneth W. Osbeck (Grand Rapids, MI: Kregel Publications, 1990), p. 324.

[46]Song used with permission of Arden Autry.

Additional copies of this book and other titles
in the *Quiet Moments with God* series and
God's Little Devotional Book series
are available at your local bookstore.

Breakfast with God
Tea Time with God
Sunset with God

God's Little Devotional Book
God's Little Devotional Book for Dads
God's Little Devotional Book for Moms
God's Little Devotional Book for Men
God's Little Devotional Book Women
God's Little Devotional Book for Students
God's Little Devotional Book for Graduates
God's Little Devotional Book for Couples

Tulsa, Oklahoma